DATE DUE			JUL 0 6
NOV 1 3 06			
GAYLORD			PRINTED IN U.S.A.

The Ruby-throated Hummingbird

NUMBER THIRTY-SIX
THE CORRIE HERRING HOOKS SERIES

Adult male Ruby-throated Hummingbird feeds at Turk's cap.
Photograph by Curtis E. Williamson.

JUNE OSBORNE

The Ruby-throated Hummingbird

THE UNIVERSITY OF TEXAS PRESS
AUSTIN

Requests for permission to reproduce material from this work
should be sent to Permissions, University of Texas Press,
Box 7819, Austin, TX 78713-7819.

∞

The paper used in this publication meets the
minimum requirements of American National Standard
for Information Sciences—Permanence of Paper for
Printed Library Materials, ANSI Z39.48-1984.

LIBRARY OF CONGRESS
CATALOGING-IN-PUBLICATION DATA

Osborne, June, 1931—
The ruby-throated hummingbird / June Osborne. —
1st University of Texas Press ed.
p.   cm. — (The Corrie Herring Hooks series ; no. 36)
Includes bibliographical references (p.   )
ISBN 0-292-76047-7
1. Ruby-throated hummingbird.   I. Title.   II. Series.
QL696.A5580735   1998
598.7'64—dc21   98-4844

This book is dedicated to the four men in my life:
my husband, Harold, whose unwavering love sustains me,
and my three sons, Mike, Van, and Sam,
whose love, devotion, and support never falter.

God seems to me more wonderful in this little bird
than in the largest animal.

Paul LeJeune, Jesuit missionary
Quebec, 1634

Contents

Preface

*T*ime and time again the tiny bird flitted away and back to the same spot on the down-sloped branch of a pecan tree in Cameron Park, Waco's largest city park. When I lifted binoculars to my eyes and focused on the bird, I discovered it was a female Ruby-throated Hummingbird. With my telescope I zoomed in on the spot she repeatedly returned to and soon realized she was working on a nest. It was so camouflaged I never would have found it had I not seen the bird's movement first. For the next six weeks I went to the park as often as I could and kept a journal of the hummer's activities until the day when her offspring successfully fledged from the nest, which ultimately was no bigger than an English walnut.

The experience of seeing that little hummer working so diligently on her nest and faithfully attending her young endeared the bird to me forever. More than a dozen years later, in the months after Shannon Davies first asked me to consider writing this book, thoughts of the hummer of Cameron Park kept leaping to the forefront of my mind, until I finally agreed to tackle the project.

I don't remember when I saw my first rubythroat. Surely, I must have seen them when I was a child growing up in Arkansas, because the Ruby-throated Hummingbird is the state's only nesting hummer, but I have no recollection of them from those days.

I first became seriously interested in the study of birds in 1975, long after I had three chicks of my own. Soon after I became addicted to bird-watching, my family began gearing our vacations to spots where we could find "new" birds. One of our first birding vacation destinations was Ramsey Canyon, Arizona, one of the prime locations in the United States to observe hummingbirds. There, in just a short time, we saw ten out of the fifteen species that nest in this country. Granted, the rubythroat was not among those hummers in southeastern

Arizona, because it regularly occurs only in the eastern half of the United States and Canada. Nevertheless, my interest in hummingbirds was enhanced by that experience.

In later years I made trips to Mexico, Costa Rica, Chile, Ecuador, and the Virgin Islands, and added many other hummingbirds to my growing list. I even traveled by chartered flight from the mainland of Chile, to a remote island in the Pacific Ocean, just to see the Juan Fernández Firecrown, a hummingbird that lives nowhere else on Earth but that one tiny island. Those trips to distant and exotic places generated a special interest in hummingbirds that no doubt had an influence on my love affair with the Ruby-throated Hummingbird, a species that I need go no farther than my own home to view.

Have you ever noticed that when things seem to be going well, life has a way of surprising us with insertions, interruptions, people we do not expect to meet, and lessons we'd rather not have to learn? Our lives are punctuated by such as these. My life is no exception.

Even though I started writing this book in the fall of 1994, I wrote the bulk of the work during the summer of 1995. My husband and I decided not to take a vacation that year so I could stay at home and work on the book. I held the grandkids at bay all summer with the excuse, "I have a deadline." My goal was to get the finished manuscript to the University of Texas Press by Christmas. Things were moving right along and it looked as if my goal would become a reality. But in the words of BettyClare Moffatt in her book *Soulwork*, "Life intervened while I was on the way to publication."

The first intervention came in November. My middle son, Van, almost died when a benign but large tumor invaded his neck. Paralysis had already crept up his left side, affecting his motor skills. After the tumor was removed, Van had full use of his hand again, but soon he had every complication in the book from the surgery. For the next five months, I helped care for my son through six more surgeries. Needless to say, during this time I had to put *The Ruby-throated Hummingbird* on hold.

During the following summer, I tried to complete the final two chapters, but life intervened again when I was diagnosed with breast cancer. The rubythroat book was forced to continue hovering in place. After a modified radical mastectomy and six months of chemotherapy, I was ready to go back to work. But then our youngest son, Sam, was diagnosed with Hodgkin's disease stage IVB. I went to Seattle to be with him through the first part of his chemotherapy.

It looked as if Fate were against the completion of this book. Then one day, as I was walking through the kitchen, I saw a small black object on our white floor. At first I thought it was a sunflower seed, but when I picked it up I discovered something far more precious. It was a hummingbird feather. It was so tiny I was afraid my breath would blow it away and I would lose it forever. I got my 10× hand lens so I could examine the feather more closely and took it to a patch of sunlight. In that infinitesimal object I saw a minute piece of the rainbow. I wish I could tell you the feather came from a Ruby-throated Hummingbird, but that would have been too good to be true. Across the surface of the feather there was a wash of deep violet, with flecks of indigo, blue, and aquamarine iridescence adding to the spectrum. It was unmistakably a gorget feather from a mature male Black-chinned Hummingbird.

How did a hummingbird feather find its way to my kitchen floor? My theory is that the bird slammed into the reflection on my storm door, knocked loose a feather or two, then flew on its way. Perhaps my son's shoe picked up the feather from the porch when he walked in. All I know is, shortly after Mike left, I found the feather.

Here, when I needed it most, was one of the grandest gifts I have ever received—a perfect piece of God's handiwork, so small and lovely I cannot find the words to describe it. This tiny microcosm of wonder that I held so reverently in my hand fought off the evil powers of darkness for me just as it did for the Aztec warriors of old. It added a flash of brightness to my day and reminded me once again that God, in all creatures great and small, pays attention to detail. How could anyone in all creation but God pack so much detail into a structure that is scarcely ten millimeters in length—little more than one-quarter of an inch! Through the simple act of picking up a speck of rainbow,

I was given light and hope to dispel the darkness of debilitating tumors, breast cancer, Hodgkin's disease, and chemotherapy. A small gift of wonder, straight from God's hand to mine, encapsulated in one tiny feather, gave me the inspiration to finish my book.

Now I ask, what shape do angels take when they come to call?

Through the pages of this book I hope to give you intimate views of all facets in the life history of this best-known of the North American hummingbirds, the Ruby-throated Hummingbird. You will learn how the female builds the nest and tends the young with no help from the male. Vicariously, you may spend a typical day with a male rubythroat that summers in Central Texas. Then see how a young female prepares herself for the incredible journey to her wintering grounds in Central America. You will find out how easy it is to attract these fascinating birds to your yard even if you have no flowers.

From Amerind legend to early explorers of the New World to colonists of New England to the present day, the Ruby-throated Hummingbird has played a part in our American culture. In fact, there is an annual celebration in Rockport-Fulton, Texas, that is dedicated to the Ruby-throated Hummingbird, making it the only species of hummer with an entire festival in its honor.

So here's to the Ruby-throated Hummingbird! May it grace our lives with its glittering beauty and its fascinating ways for a long time to come.

Acknowledgments

*I*t would be impossible to tackle such a project as this alone. I am grateful to my sponsoring editor, Shannon Davies, for her endless patience and her expert guidance. Without her constant words of encouragement this work would never have seen the light of day.

My husband, Harold, provided unwavering support and constructive criticism through his numerous readings of the manuscript.

My splendid, devoted friend Sharlande Sledge donned her English-teacher hat and read and proofread the final draft with red pen in hand.

Ellie Womack was extremely helpful, especially while I was writing the chapter on hummingbird banding. She and I e-mailed the pages back and forth to each other many times until I finally got it right.

Nancy Newfield provided needed information and gave encouragement, and she allowed me to hold in my hands and release one of the rubythroats she banded at the "Hummer/ Bird Celebration!" in Rockport-Fulton, Texas.

I am indebted to Janet Sheets, who retrieved documents both in the scientific field and in the popular literature from the archives of Moody Library, Baylor University, in Waco.

Last, but by no means least, I owe a tremendous debt of gratitude to photographers Curtis E. Williams, Luke Wade, Barbara Garland, Beth K. Hawkins, and Alan Murphy for the brilliant images they contributed to make this book a work of art.

"Little birds . . . so different from ours it is a marvel."

Christopher Columbus, October 21, 1492

ONE

Hummingbirds: Their Human Appeal

*H*ummingbirds, like Wild Turkeys, are true native Americans. They live only in the Americas. Can you imagine the awe and amazement when Columbus and the first European visitors set foot on land in the Indies and glimpsed their first hummingbirds? They were like no other bird the explorers had ever seen and certainly were beyond any bird they had ever imagined. The feisty little birds (not much bigger than some insects) must have seemed surprisingly small to the awestruck observers. They had feathers that glowed and actually changed colors at the slightest turn of the head or body, and they seemed to fly at the speed of light. Furthermore, not only could they fly frontward, backward, up, down, side to side, and upside down, but they could even stand still in midair. I'm sure the explorers were totally enchanted by the aerial antics of these intriguing little birds. Is it any wonder that hummers were the source of great interest and folklore for the earliest visitors to the New World?

These pioneer bird-watchers were so taken with the mystifying birds that they were eager to send word of the "flying marvels" to friends and family, so they took pen in hand to relate the new discoveries to those back home. But how to describe them, and what to call them? They had no name to ascribe to the unfamiliar flying jewels, so they used some of the names their new Indian friends used. Most of them were almost impossible to pronounce, much less to translate into terms that could be understood in Europe. Nevertheless, descriptions of these fascinating small creatures soon appeared in letters, journals, and official reports.

Undoubtedly, Christopher Columbus was the first European of note to make mention of the avian wonders. He, too, found it difficult to describe them. The entry in his travel journal on October 21, 1492, said rather simply: "Little birds . . . so different from ours it is a marvel." No doubt, it was Columbus himself who took back to Europe the first dried specimens of hummingbirds so those at home could see for themselves these tiny marvels.

A Hummer by Any Other Name

In their letters back home, the Spanish explorers gave hummers imaginative and picturesque names in their own language. Four of the most popular were: *picaflor,* meaning "flower piercer"; *chupaflor,* "flower sucker" or "sipper"; and *chuparrosa* or *chupamyrto,* "sucker of roses and myrtle." Even today those are the four names most often heard in Spanish-speaking countries of Middle America. Another charming and descriptive Spanish name is *joyas voladores,* "flying jewels." In Brazil, where Portuguese is the language, early settlers coined the name *chupamel,* "honey sipper." The lovely Portuguese name that is still used today is *beija-flor,* "flower kisser."

Pietro Martire de Anghiera was an Italian scholar who served Queen Isabella as diplomatic envoy and tutor to young court pages. In that capacity he had access to all the written reports from returned voyagers describing these unbelievable birds. He noted that the voyagers, one and all, marveled that there could be a bird tinier than the ones Europeans had always regarded as the smallest birds in the world, the kinglet and the wren (both called regolo), at 3.5 to 4 inches, bill to tail.

Just over a century later, the first English-born American to write about hummingbirds was none other than Captain John Smith, one of the founders of Jamestown Colony in Virginia and the colony's chief historian. The first of his several volumes was published in London in 1608. It was followed in 1624 by a general history of Virginia, New England, and Bermuda. Even though he didn't say so, the bird of which he wrote was surely the Ruby-throated Hummingbird, since it is the only one that is seen regularly east of the Mississippi River. Of course, at that point in time the bird had not been officially named. Smith was

An adult male rubythroat is not much bigger than this Gulf fritillary.
Photograph by Curtis E. Williams.

enchanted by the bird's small size and described it as "Scarce so big as a wren and less than a kinglet," two familiar birds to which he knew Europeans could relate.

No one knows for sure who came up with the name "hummingbird," but it was almost certainly first applied to the Ruby-throated Hummingbird by English colonists on the eastern seaboard of North America. Thus the name by which we know the entire family of Trochilidae was first bestowed on the rubythroat, a species with exceptionally sonorous flight. Had English-speaking people first seen living hummingbirds in the tropics, where many fly more silently, we would probably know them today by a different name.

By sometime in the 1630s, "hum bird" and "humming bird" were in use in the colonists' speech, and "hummer" soon followed. William Wood first used Humbird on the printed page in his book *New Englands Prospects,* published in London in 1634: "For colour shee is glorious as the Rainebowe, as shee flies shee makes a little humming noise like a humble bee; wherefore shee is called Humbird." Wood traveled to Massachusetts Colony in 1630, wrote the book, and returned to England to see it published. Wood's Humbird was the rubythroat, since it is the only one with which he could have had contact. And so, the Ruby-throated Hummingbird became one of the first avian species celebrated in American literature.

The French called it *oiseau mouche*—a bird with the quality of a fly. In Quebec in 1634, a Jesuit missionary, Paul Le Jeune, wrote of *oiseau mouche* but declared that it should be translated as "flower bird" rather than "fly bird." He said the hummer was "one of the rarities of the country and a little prodigy of nature."

No matter what one labels these marvels of the bird world— *picaflor, beija-flor, chuparrosa, chupamel, oiseau mouche*—they are truly *joyas voladores,* "flying jewels," that continue to charm observers today even as they did European explorers more than 500 years ago.

COMMON NAMES

Since the rubythroat was the only species in eastern North America, it was *the* species of the English colonists. They first used "northern" and "red-throated" as modifiers to designate the species in common terms. Later, John James Audubon and Thomas Nuttall, ornithologists of the late eighteenth and early nineteenth centuries, gave the bird the common name by which we know it today, "Ruby-throated Hummingbird," for its red gorget (throat patch).

In Mexico it is sometimes called *chupamirto de fuego,* "myrtle sipper color of fire." Other names it has been called are "common hummingbird" and "rubythroat." Hummingbirds were once known as kingbirds, for the regal way in which they put other birds to flight.

The Cherokee people of the southeastern United States knew the rubythroat as *tsa-lu tsi-skwa*, "tobacco bringer." Legend has it that suddenly tobacco vanished from the land of the Cherokee and none could be found. Since the people used tobacco for medicinal purposes as well as for pleasure and important tribal ceremonies, they missed it sorely. The tale relates that their beloved elder became ill, and nothing could ease his pain but tobacco. Finally, a medicine man who could magically turn himself into a hummingbird volunteered to go and search for the precious life-saving leaves. Sure enough, the little bird found them and brought back not only leaves but also seeds for re-planting. Their elder was saved from an untimely death, and once again the people had tobacco.

Comte Georges-Louis Leclerc de Buffon, the most famous French naturalist of the eighteenth century, insisted on using French instead of Latin to describe birds. His name for the Ruby-throated Hummingbird was simply Le Rubis, "the Ruby."

SCIENTIFIC NAMES

Scientific classification of plants and animals as we know it today actually began in biblical times when Moses set down the features that determined if animals were or were not fit for food (Leviticus 11 and Deuteronomy 14). The ancient Hebrew laws set down in the Old Testament aligned animals by habitat—as creatures of land, water, or air—and as clean or unclean. Much later, Carolus Linnaeus, the famous eighteenth-century botanist of Sweden, patterned his modern-era scientific method of classifying plants and animals after those Hebrew laws. Linnaeus is recognized worldwide today as the father of taxonomy. His system gives each individual type of plant or animal a name and a meaningful place in relation to others of the same general sort.

One of the original species Linnaeus listed in his tenth edition of *Systema Naturae* in 1758 was the Ruby-throated Hum-

Unlike other birds, hummingbirds move their wings only at the shoulder. Photograph by Luke Wade.

mingbird, which he called *Trochilus Colubris.* Since he had never seen the bird in person, he based the name on descriptions of the species published by Mark Catesby and George Edwards, two naturalists of the early eighteenth century. The bird was reclassified in 1854 as *Archilochus* by Ludwig Reichenbach, director of the Dresden Zoological Museum. Almost a century and a half later the name still stands. The Ruby-throated Hummingbird is officially known in scientific circles today as *Archilochus colubris*, and there are no known subspecies.

Archilochus is Greek for "chief brigand." It was coined from *archos,* meaning "chief," or "first in importance," and *lochus,* "ambush" or "a company of men." It is thought that Reichenbach chose this Latin word because the bird steals pollen from flowers and then dashes away. The term *colubris* is the Latinized form of a South American Indian word for these birds, *colibri*. The Taino people of the Bahamas were the first tribe encountered by Christopher Columbus in the New World. They translated *colibri* to mean "sky spirit," "magic sky bird," "god bird," or "sun god bird."

The Rubythroat as Icon

Further testimony of the hummingbird's appeal to humans is our use of it as an icon on the objects of beauty that surround our daily lives. From the time the first sagamores greeted the Puritan colonists on the shores of New England, the Ruby-throated Hummingbird has decorated our lives in many ways. Those great men among the American Indians wore the beautiful little birds as ear adornments, actually making earrings of the birds. Not just a likeness of the bird but the entire body of the bird dangled from their earlobes. Its iridescent feathers were considered a great thing of beauty to be flaunted.

Rubythroat skins were so revered in those days, they were exclusively reserved for the tribal leaders. In Mexico, the Aztec war god was recognized by the bracelet of dazzling hummingbird feathers on his left wrist. Members of Aztec royal families wore cloaks of glittering hummingbird feathers. Later, in the nineteenth century, rubythroat skins, as well as those of other hummingbirds, were in high demand to be used as decorations on women's hats, bags, jewelry, fans, and gowns in Europe and in the New World.

Athletic teams all over the United States and Canada have chosen many different birds as their mascots or symbols, from eagles to roadrunners to cardinals; however, I find no record of any athletic team choosing the Ruby-throated Hummingbird as a mascot. In my opinion it would be a good bird to choose because of its agility and speed of flight. Imagine the headlines after a game between the North Carolina Ruby-throated Hummingbirds and the St. Louis Cardinals: "The Hummers have done it again! 'So and so' knocked that ball right out of the stadium. It went sailing through the air as if on gossamer wings." Even though they are not chosen as athletic icons, today one may walk into almost any gift shop and see Ruby-throated Hummingbird likenesses on many, many objects, from stationery and greeting cards to fine works of art. I have composed a list of all the objects on which I can remember seeing some rendition of the Ruby-throated Hummingbird: stationery, notecards, greeting cards, dishes, mugs, candle holders, candles, Christmas ornaments, clocks, wristwatches, wind chimes, socks, T-shirts, women's blouses, scarves, button covers, doormats, mailboxes, house numbers, tiles, stepping stones, lampshades, decorative name plaques, all kinds of jewelry (including pins, bracelets, earrings, charms, and necklaces), light switchplates, wind socks, weather vanes, ornamental flags, magnets, quilling art, sun catchers, blown-glass figurines, porcelain figurines, keychains, wood carvings, faucet handles, rubber stamps, jigsaw puzzles, thermometers, placemats, napkins, handpainted handbags and tote bags, bars of soap, calendars, needlepoint and embroidery, blankets, bookmarks, coloring books, and of course, bird books and fine works of art. In fact, many of these objects decorate my own home.

The United States Post Office even got into the act. In 1992 it issued a series of first-class postage stamps portraying five different species of hummers: Ruby-throated, Broad-billed, Costa's, Rufous, and Calliope Hummingbirds. One of America's leading artists, Don Balke, was chosen to design the stamps. From his home in rural Wisconsin he had ample opportunity to study his subjects, especially the rubythroat. His painstaking attention to detail is obvious in his work for the Official National Audubon Society Hummingbirds Collection.

From the official proofcard for the rubythroat stamp I quote: "No other bird has captured the imagination of mankind as completely as the hummingbird. Birdwatchers are enraptured by the little birds, with their bright coloration, extraordinary flying antics and minute size. The artwork on this Proofcard and accompanying stamp salutes the Ruby-throated Humming-bird, captivating gem of the East."

As you can see, hummingbirds hold a fascination for humans that cannot be matched by any other family of birds. Besides all the reasons already mentioned, hummingbirds give us many chances to view them. Since they live in the fast lane, so to speak, and must eat often to survive, they are among the earliest of birds to rise in the morning and among the latest to retire in the evening. From early in the day to late evening, throughout their breeding season, they are all about us in our gardens, buzzing around our flowers or our hummingbird feeders. No wonder we are so enthralled by them. Robert Ridgway summed it up best: hummers are, without doubt, "the most remarkable group of birds in the entire world."

"Inhabitants exclusively of America, the Humming Birds constitute not only the most charming element in the wonderfully varied birdlife of the Western Hemisphere, but, also, without doubt, the most remarkable group of birds in the entire world."

Robert Ridgway, bird curator, Smithsonian Institution
(1869–1880)

TWO

A Family of Tiny Dynamos

There's no doubt about it. Hummingbirds are among the most fascinating creatures on Earth. Almost everyone enjoys watching their antics. What is it about hummingbirds that so captivates *Homo sapiens*? Everything about these dynamos of nature is out of the ordinary. Their diminutive size defies human logic. The variety of their colors and patterns is kaleidoscopic. Their tiny crops can store enough food to sustain them through the night. Their slender, pointed bills are adapted for probing particular flowers for nectar. They have the greatest energy output of all the warm-blooded animals. Their ability to become dormant at night allows them to endure drastic changes in temperature. Their maneuverability in flight appears to defy gravity. Their long-distance migrations seem unthinkable for creatures of their size. In short, the hummingbird challenges the limits of human perception and understanding.

Indeed, for all those distinctive qualities and more, humans are enchanted by this family of birds in an order of its own, Trochiliformes, and family Trochilidae. It is the largest of the nonpasserine (nonsongbird) families and the second largest avian family in the Western Hemisphere—second only to the tyrant flycatchers (Tyrannidae), which have more than 370 species. Recent classifiers have placed this family of birds (Trochilidae) at the very head of the nonpasserines as the most highly evolved of the 28 nonpasserine orders.

Scientists have identified more than 340 species of hummingbirds and 116 genera, and they are still counting. Every few years someone discovers a new species somewhere in the tropics. At least six new species have been identified since 1970. Our American hummingbirds—those that can be seen north of the Mexican border—belong to 10 out of the 116 genera.

Hummingbirds live solely in the Western Hemisphere, from Alaska to Tierra del Fuego. More than half the hummingbird species live in South America along the equatorial belt, which is 10 degrees wide. Oddly enough, it is the Andes, not the Amazon basin as one might expect, that supports the greatest hummingbird diversity. A few of the hardiest species live at altitudes above 15,000 feet, where the air is thin and the temperature quickly falls below freezing after the sun sets. On a trip to Ecuador in 1997, I saw one of them, the Andean Hillstar, at Cotopaxi National Park. At night this remarkable little bird finds shelter in a rock crevice, where it lowers its body temperature from a normal 104°F to 59°F in order to survive the freezing night temperatures at such altitudes.

Colombia has the most hummingbird species of any country, with more than 140. Ecuador and Peru are next with around 120 each. I have seen 33 species of the hummers in South America. Here their splendor of plumage is reflected in such common names as "Sparkling Violet-ear," "Andean Emerald," "Fawn-breasted Brilliant," "Shining Sunbeam," "White-bellied Woodstar," and "Gorgeted Sunangel." Tierra del Fuego has only one species, the Green-backed Firecrown. The Juan Fernández Firecrown *(Sephanoides fernandensis)* is endemic to the Juan Fernández Archipelago and lives nowhere else in the world but on one remote island in the South Pacific, Isla Robinson Crusoe, 400 miles from Chile's mainland. I was privileged to go there in 1993 and photographed the bird.

North of the equator, from Panama to Mexico, there are more than 50 species of hummingbirds. North America north of the Mexican border claims 15 species of hummingbirds that occur on a regular basis. Five of those, including the Ruby-throated Hummingbird, are found in Canada.

Although no fossil imprints of these delicate birds have been discovered, Alan Feduccia states in *The Age of Birds* that hummingbirds are "almost certainly of post-Cretaceous origin because of their South American distribution." It seems logical to believe that hummers evolved after the appearance of flowering plants in the Cretaceous period. Alexander Skutch, in *The Life of the Hummingbird*, says, "That the family is ancient is attested by its many species and wide dispersion over the Western Hemisphere, where doubtless it originated." So you see, humming-birds have been around for a long, long time and, apparently, have always been exclusively in the Western Hemisphere.

Size

Hummingbirds are the Lilliputians of the bird world. The small-est of them all, and the smallest bird in the world, is the male Cuban Bee Hummingbird *(Mellisuga helenae)* that measures 2 to 2.25 inches in length, and half of that is bill and tail. The female is about a quarter of an inch longer. It tips the scales at just 2 grams. That is slightly more than one-fifteenth of an ounce—less than the weight of a penny. The largest in weight, not in length, is the Giant Hummingbird *(Patagona gigas)* of the South American Andes. At 8.5 inches, it is about 2 inches shorter than the streamertails and the Black-tailed Trainbearer.

Unlike most other birds, female hummingbirds are larger than males in the smaller species and males are larger in the larger species. The Ruby-throated Hummingbird averages 3.75 inches in length, from bill tip to tail tip—"not even as long as a Bald Eagle's middle toe," according to Virginia Holmgren. It weighs a whopping 3.34 grams, about one-tenth the weight of a first-class letter. It takes approximately 160 rubythroats to make one pound. Its wingspan is only 4.25 inches, and yet it can fly nonstop over 600 miles of open water in migration, a marathon journey that takes from ten to eighteen hours.

Even though hummingbirds are the smallest of all birds, they are probably the most active. Their wings beat 10 to 80 times per second (depending on the species), and they must feed ev-ery ten to fifteen minutes to keep up their energy levels.

Hummingbirds have by far the largest hearts relative to body size. Among all birds, the smaller the species, the larger the heart proportionately. The smaller species of hummingbirds have proportionately larger hearts than the bigger ones. The weight of a hummingbird's heart ranges from approximately 1.75 per-cent to 2.5 percent of its total body weight. Relatively large hearts are necessary for hummingbirds to cope with their extremely rapid metabolism and their method of feeding from flower to flower, which sometimes requires them to fly great distances in a given day. In proportion to body weight, a hummingbird's heart is six times larger than a human's heart. The heart of an adult male Ruby-throated Hummingbird beats about 200 to 600 times per minute, but that rate can escalate to around 1,200 beats per minute while the bird is feeding or if it is agitated. By comparison, an adult human, at rest, has an average heart rate of 72 beats per minute. The brains of hummingbirds are among the relatively largest of all birds as well. The brain comprises at least 4.2 percent of the hummingbird's body weight. So count it a compliment if someone calls you a birdbrain, especially if that someone is referring to a hummingbird's brain.

Most hummingbirds' feet are so small that some people think they don't even have them. Indeed, while the tiny birds are in flight they hold their feet so close to their bodies that they become almost invisible. Their feet are certainly not made for walking or hopping. In fact, most species of hummingbirds cannot walk at all. In order to shift position on a limb or on the nest, the bird simply rises in the air an inch or two and alights again in a new position.

So what are hummingbird feet designed for? They have been described as "retractable landing gear." They are for perching on small twigs and wires. Their toes are well developed for this purpose, with three toes directed forward and one backward. They are used for preening and scratching what itches. Most hummingbirds scratch the same way most passerines (songbirds) do—by lifting one foot up and over the wing. Of course, the female hummer uses her feet to arrange nesting materials.

In a family so large as the hummingbird family, one would expect that there might be a few exceptions to the rule. Alexander Skutch relates some of these exceptions in *The Life of the Hummingbird*. He reports that in Bolivia, at 15,000 feet above sea level, François Vuilleumier observed an Olivaceous Thornbill *(Chalcostigma olivaceum)* as it hopped across the thickly mat-

While in flight, hummingbirds hold their feet close to their bodies.
Photograph by Curtis E. Williams.

ted grass of a meadow and picked up insects it found there. Similar terrestrial foraging has been reported of the Bearded Helmetcrest *(Oxypogon guerinii)* and a few other related species of the high Andes as well.

The Juan Fernández Firecrown (the hummingbird that lives only on Isla Robinson Crusoe in the South Pacific) has exceptionally large feet, which it uses to cling to the blossoms from which it feeds. It hangs upside down while feeding.

Colors

John James Audubon once described a hummingbird as a "glittering garment of the rainbow." The English ornithologist John Gould called hummers "wonderful works of creation." In more recent times, Pete Dunne, director of the Cape May Bird Observatory in New Jersey, declares that hummers "humble the colors of the rainbow." Granted, the iridescent colors of hummingbirds are dazzling to the eye. It is almost impossible to describe hummingbirds without using superlatives or comparing them to jewels. Indeed, they are often referred to as the "flying jewels of summer."

For as long as humans have watched these little avian gems, they have compared them to jewels and named them for those they best depict. Consider some of the names that have been ascribed to hummingbirds: White-bellied Emerald, Purple-throated Mountain-gem, Sapphire-throated Hummingbird, Fork-tailed Emerald, Glittering Emerald, Emerald Woodnymph, Sapphire-spangled Emerald, Great Sapphirewing, Ruby-topaz Hummingbird, Amethyst-throated Hummingbird, Garnet-throated Hummingbird, and Ruby-throated Hummingbird—well, you get the picture. The list goes on and on. The names alone conjure up intensely colorful mental images.

The Kwakiutl called the hummer *k-waak-umtia,* "bird with face painted by sun." The Mayas' descriptive name was *xo-ma-xamil,* meaning "many-colored" or "bird of gold with throat of fire." The Aztec called them *huitzili, huitzitzil,* or *uitzitzil,* "shining one with the weapon (its beak) like a cactus thorn."

The ancient Amerind people were poetic with their descriptions. The feathers of hummers do glitter and shine as if "painted by the sun," and they change colors at the slightest movement of the head or body. At one moment the gorget (throat patch) of a male Ruby-throated Hummingbird looks black. At the turn of its head, when the light strikes it at just the right angle, it is almost as if a light turns on inside its throat, for suddenly the black throat feathers are transformed to glittering ruby red.

More than once I have demonstrated this point for groups

of schoolchildren with the study skin of a male Ruby-throated Hummingbird. I held the tiny specimen in my hand and showed them how the feathers on the gorget are magically transformed simply by turning the bird's body toward the light. Of all the birds I show to schoolchildren, invariably, the tiny humming-birds intrigue them most. After one such session, a third-grader wrote me a letter in which she stated, "I especially liked the redlight hummingbird."

You may ask how hummingbirds execute those dramatic changes in color. Is it magic? Sometimes it actually seems so. In Aztec legend, every warrior who died in battle was magically turned into a hummingbird and rewarded with a time of ease in the flower-filled gardens of paradise. Here the warriors enjoyed sweet nectar as their daily food. When needed they were turned back into warriors, and they were warned to remain ever ready for battle. Each evening at dusk Huitzitzilo-pochtli called on them to help fight off the evil powers of darkness. The Aztecs feared that without this nightly defense, darkness might en-velop the earth for all time and deprive the world of the sun's warmth and golden light.

The hummer warriors rallied for battle to ensure the sun's appearance in full glory each morning. During winter, when the shadows of night remained on the earth for longer periods of time, the hummer warriors had to fight all the harder if the sun was to return. The legend says that the sun rewarded the hummers for their strength, courage, and skill—every time they faced the sun their feathers were to be "touched with golden radiance" and their gorgets to appear as "jewels set in gold."

Perhaps what appears to be magic or the stuff of legend may be explained rather simply. In order to understand this miracu-lous change of color, someone suggested blowing some bubbles and watching their colors change as they float through the air. Then imagine a million tiny bubbles stacked together to give some idea of how the hummingbird's feathers work. Author Timothy Levi Biel suggests, "If you could magnify a humming-bird's feather, you would see that parts of it are covered with thousands of tiny *'bubbles.'* These *bubbles* have various shapes and thicknesses, so light bounces off them at different angles. And when light bounces at different *angles,* it appears as different *colors.*"

It is almost as if each tiny feather has a built-in prism that refracts the light in brilliant hues. Actually, each iridescent feather has tiny ridges and platelets, so they reflect colors according to the angle of light.

Some species of hummingbirds have these sparkling colors only on their throats. Others sport them on their heads, throats, and backs. In most species it is only the male that is adorned with such scintillating colors. In a few species, however, the female is just as dazzling as the male. The male and female Green Violet-ear *(Colibri thalassinus)* are alike, except the female is slightly duller than the male. In the Buff-bellied Hummingbird (*Amazilia yucatanensis*), the sexes are alike, and Berylline Hummingbirds *(Amazilia beryllina)* are alike except for their lower bellies. The male berylline's belly is chestnut and the female's is grayish. These are just three examples. In fact, in approximately one-third of the world's hummingbirds, we find that the female's plumage is equally as splendid as the male's.

A few species of hummingbirds are not so blessed with dazzling colors, for a good reason. The more brightly colored hummers live mostly in sunny areas where they blend with their surroundings, but the duller ones, mostly the hermits, live in shaded underbrush where their cryptic coloration makes them better fitted for concealment.

Bill

Long, slender, pointed bills, perhaps more than any other single feature, distinguish hummingbirds from all other birds. Their bills may be straight or decurved (curved downward), or even recurved (curved upward). Bills may be short, very short, long, or very long. Most hummingbird bills are at least as long as their heads are wide. Most are longer. They range in length from five-sixteenths of an inch in the Purple-backed Thornbill *(Ramphomicron microrhynchum),* whose bill is not even as long as its head, to the four-inch bill of the Sword-billed Humming-bird *(Ensifera ensifera)*, which is almost as long as its entire body.

The adaptive variations of hummingbirds' bills are manifold. These multiple variations reflect the adaptation of each species to its particular feeding habits. The long bill enables the bird to probe deep into the throats of tubular flowers for the life-giving nectar within. In fact, the bills of different species are adapted for feeding on particular kinds of flowers, which is the primary reason why so many different species can coexist in the tropics. For example, the sharply downcurved bill of the White-tipped Sicklebill *(Eutoxeres aquila)* makes it one of the few hummingbirds capable of feeding from the hook-shaped heliconia. The extremely long bill of the Long-tailed Hermit *(Phaethornis superciliosus)* makes it one of the few hummingbirds able to get nectar out of a scarlet passionflower. The half-inch bill of the Bearded Helmetcrest *(Oxypogon guerinii)* is one of the shortest bills of all. The swordbill, that amazing hummer of the high Andes of South America, with its four-inch bill gathers nectar from a number of plant species that are characterized by very deep trumpet-shaped flowers.

Hummingbirds use their bills not only for feeding on nectar and insects but also to preen their feathers and to attack other hummingbirds. In Rockport, Texas, I watched two female rubythroats as they tried to feed from the same feeder. The first one there chased the second one away as soon as she arrived. The chase ended in what appeared to be a duel, as the two of them went beak to beak from a height of about fifteen feet in the air all the way to the ground. They landed on a rock beneath the feeder, where they struggled a few seconds, and the aggressor seemed to stab the intruder in the back with her bill. As soon as she flew away, the victim, which I thought was surely dead, shook herself all over, rose up, and went after the attacker with a vengeance. Is it any wonder the Aztecs called the hummer Shining One with the Weapon Like a Cactus Thorn?

Of course, the female hummer uses her bill to gather nesting materials, construct the nest, catch flying insects, and feed her young.

Tongue

A hummingbird's long, extensible tongue is about twice the length of the bill and is forked on the end. When at rest, it fits within the hummingbird's beak. The base of the tongue is attached to thin tissue at the back of the throat, and it winds up inside the back of the head, much like a woodpecker's tongue. It's almost as if the tongue is on a spring. When the bill opens, the tissue extends and allows the tongue to flick forward. When the tissue contracts, the nectar-filled tongue returns. Hummingbird tongues have small wavy membranes on the sides to soak up the nectar. They actually lap up the nectar from a flower by licking, at the rate of thirteen licks per second, much the same as a cat laps up a bowl of milk. Contrary to former belief, a hummingbird's tongue is not like a soda straw through which it sucks nectar into its mouth. Rather, it is now believed that nectar is drawn into the tongue by means of capillary action and is swallowed after the tongue is retracted into the mouth and squeezed.

The outer half of a hummingird's tongue has fringed edges that may help the bird catch minute insects found inside flowers.

Did you know that hummingbirds have taste receptors and salivary glands on their tongues? Yes, they can taste the sweetness of the nectar, and they have taste preferences much the same as humans do. They habitually return to feeders and flowers that offer sweet rewards. They reject nectar that is less than 12 percent sugar, which equals the sweetness of a popular cola soft drink. They even seem to abhor the taste of certain plants such as oleander, which is poisonous to humans.

Metabolism

Hummingbirds, the smallest birds in the world, have the highest rate of metabolism, the process by which food is turned into energy. Because of their size and lifestyle, they have the greatest energy output, relatively, of any warm-blooded animal, except perhaps the shrew, a tiny mouselike mammal. That's why hummingbirds have to eat so often—five to eight times each hour—to keep up their energy level. On an average day, for instance, a Ruby-throated Hummingbird may have to visit as many as 1,500 flowers to meet its daily dietary requirements. Individual hummingbirds often consume more than half their total weight in food every day, and they may drink about twice their weight in water per day.

If humans had the same weight-specific metabolic rate as a hummingbird, their temperature might reach 750°F, and they would need to consume about 155,000 calories and drink 100 gallons of water every day. If a normal man's energy output were equivalent to that of a hummer, he would have to consume, in one day, 285 pounds of hamburger or 370 pounds of boiled potatoes or 130 pounds of bread. Humans normally eat about 2 to 3 pounds of food daily.

A woman in Iowa conducted a fascinating experiment, feeding wild Ruby-throated Hummingbirds in her back yard over a period of seven years. She determined that each hummingbird ate a total of one teaspoonful of sugar every day. That is about one and one-half times the weight of each bird. If a man who weighed 200 pounds ate sugar at the same rate that hummers do, he would eat 300 pounds of sugar every day.

A third-grader who attended one of my school bird programs was asked what he remembered most about my presentation. His classic reply was, "Hummingbirds travel a lot and eat a lot."

Torpor

Have you ever wondered how such a tiny creature as a hummingbird could possibly survive sudden changes in the weather? The answer is, hummingbirds are capable of entering a state of reduced metabolic function at night called torpor. This means that their body activity levels lower to approximate, roughly, hibernation in the mammal world. Their body temperature, which normally ranges from 104° to 110°F, in torpor drops to between 60° and 70°F. Their heart rate slows to about 50 beats per minute, their metabolic rate lowers to about one-fifth the normal rate, and their breathing (normally 250 breaths per minute while at rest) becomes irregular and sometimes stops altogether for brief periods of time. Indeed, sometimes hummingbirds appear to be dead in such a state. Perhaps this is why in Amerind legend the hummingbird was known as the resurrection bird. Sometimes a tribal woman of long ago would pick up a torpid hummingbird and place it in her bosom until the bird warmed sufficiently to come back to life and fly away.

Coming out of torpor can take up to one hour, depending on surrounding conditions. If the sun is out, it warms the bird's body as it warms the air in the morning. If a person takes the bird in hand to warm it, or if some other artificial source of warmth is used, the bird's temperature may rise rapidly. Upon awakening, its heartbeat and breathing rates increase until the body temperature rises to at least 86°F, at which time it is able to fly.

There is one bodily function that is not affected by torpidity—the grasping reflex that helps a bird stay on its perch while sleeping. This function remains as strong while the bird is in torpor as it is while the bird's body temperature is at its normal level. This is a definite advantage for hummers, which might otherwise fall off their perches when they go into torpor.

By becoming torpid a hummingbird simply reduces its need for food. It is not necessary for hummingbirds to resort to torpor every night; it is only a last resort, used in an emergency when their energy reserves are so low that they need to conserve energy in order to survive the night. It's a lot like changing the thermostat at night to save on the electric bill.

Whether a hummingbird goes into torpor depends not only on the ambient temperature but also on the bird's overall condition as well. Is the bird well nourished, or does it have dietary deficiencies? Is it in good health or ill health? Are its food reserves sufficient or insufficient to sustain it through the night? Also, female hummers never become torpid while they are incubating eggs or while brooding nestlings. Neither do older nestlings enter torpidity when left exposed. In either case, if their temperature is allowed to fall to a low enough level, the development of embryos and nestlings will be dangerously retarded.

Flight

In the bird world, hummingbirds are the undisputed champions of the sky. They are true flying acrobats. Indeed, they maneuver more like helicopters than other birds, whose flight more nearly mimics that of rigid-winged gasbirds. Igor Sikorsky, the helicopter's inventor, said he got his best design ideas for the whirlybird from watching hummingbirds in flight.

Hummingbirds are capable of performing tricks in the air that no other bird can match. They can fly forward, backward, up, down, side to side, and, yes, even upside down. The hummingbird's tail acts as a rudder to steer the bird in flight. Furthermore, hummers can hover. Of course, hovering is one of their most outstanding attributes—the ability to remain suspended in midair, as if sitting on an invisible perch, while they feed at a flower blossom or a hummingbird feeder. The only aerial maneuver hummingbirds are incapable of is soaring; however, some of the larger species are capable of gliding for considerable distances, like swifts. Even some smaller species occasionally glide for a split second.

Not surprisingly, about one-quarter of a hummingbird's weight is in its chest muscles, the bird's largest muscles. They are needed to power its magnificent flight. The hefty pectoral (chest) muscle of the Ruby-throated Hummingbird powers the bird on its flight thousands of miles from southern Canada, for instance, southward to the Yucatan Peninsula and farther.

All birds have two chest muscles—one for the upstroke and one for the downstroke. Most other birds have relatively tiny muscles for raising their wings, and all their flying power comes from the downstroke. But in hummingbirds, the flight muscles are so large and strong that the bird gets flying power from both the upstroke and the downstroke. Hummingbird muscles

Hummers can even fly upside down.
Photograph by Curtis E. Williams.

that provide power on the upstroke are relatively larger than those of other birds but still weigh only half that of the down-stroke muscles.

As you might guess, their powerful flight muscles are supported by an oversized breastbone, by far the largest bone in a hummingbird's body. If you could see the skeleton of a hummingbird, you would be amazed at the size of this bone relative to all its other bones. Dwarfed by the breastbone's magnitude, the others, by comparison, look smaller than toothpicks.

The design of a hummingbird's wing is unique among birds. Whereas other birds move their wings at the shoulder, elbow, and wrist, hummingbirds move theirs only at the shoulder, which swivels in a joint more like the partial spin of a helicopter rotor blade than a conventional wing. The hummingbird's entire wing acts as a propeller, which is why most of them are incapable of soaring or gliding. On the other hand, this is precisely why they have such tremendous maneuverability in flight.

Many kinds of birds are capable of hovering. What can be more thrilling than seeing an Osprey, seemingly motionless above its prey, before it dives on a fish in the water a hundred feet below? Or perhaps you have watched a kingfisher stand still in the air before folding its wings and splashing down to retrieve a tiny minnow, or a White-tailed Kite hanging in midair as if suspended on invisible string before diving on a mouse. All these and a few other birds certainly are adept at hovering flight. Each poises and holds its position in the air against the downward pull of gravity by beating its wings up and down and depressing and spreading its tail feathers until ready to dive on its prey. These birds accomplish this feat by flying into the wind at a velocity that is equal to the speed of the wind.

Hummingbirds, above all other birds, are undoubtedly the most skilled at the feat of hovering and really are the only birds that are true hoverers. One unique thing about hummingbirds is that they can turn their wings completely upside down on the backstroke, thus producing a horizontal figure-eight pattern at the wing tip. Essentially, what happens is that the downstroke cancels out the upstroke and leaves the bird motionless. John K. Terres (in *The Audubon Society Encyclopedia of North American Birds*) describes it this way: "The hummingbird *hovers* by rotating its shoulder joint and turning its pointed wings completely over on the backstroke and the forestroke, which cut through the air and check the tendency to move forward or backward."

But why, you may ask, must a hummingbird hover? No one knows for sure the whole story, but one reason may be that many flowers hummingbirds visit for sustenance provide no opportunity to perch. Besides, hovering makes it possible for the tiny dynamos to move more quickly between flowers, and some of them must visit as many as 1,500 flowers in one day to survive. No matter what the reasons are for hovering, it is truly one of the marvels of ornithology.

The smaller species of hummingbirds have the most rapid wingbeat of all birds. In forward flight they beat their wings up to 80 times a second, 55 times a second while hovering, and 61 times a second when backing up. Perhaps this is why we view these enchanting birds as gossamer clouds of humming wings. In flight a hummingbird's wings are visible only as a blur.

Surprisingly, the rate of some hummingbirds' wingbeats is actually slower than that of some other larger-winged birds. For example, the Northern Mockingbird beats its wings about 14 times per second, and the Giant Hummingbird, which is smaller than the mockingbird, beats its wings about 8 to 10 times per second. I believe it, because the Giant Hummingbirds I have observed, once in Chile and once in Ecuador, flew more like butterflies than hummingbirds. They seemed to float slowly and gracefully from one agave bloom to the next. This is one more proof that the wingbeat of hummingbirds is more efficient than the wingbeat of other birds simply because their power is generated on both the upstroke and the downstroke.

Hummingbirds are among the fastest fliers of the small birds. They can fly circles around most other birds, so they have little fear of predators. To protect their nests, these feisty little birds have been known to attack eagles. Female rubythroats have been clocked at 27 miles per hour in a wind tunnel, at 45 to 60 miles per hour in forward flight along a highway, and up to 65 miles per hour in dives.

A hummingbird wing has ten primary feathers, which are extremely long and narrow. When the wings flap, these feathers vibrate, causing the humming sound that gives the bird its name. (And I thought they hummed because they couldn't remember the words of the song!)

With the combination of unusually strong muscles and efficient wing design, is it any wonder the hummingbird provided Sikorsky with ideas for the design of the first helicopter? There's no doubt about it. In flight, no other bird comes close to a hummingbird. It reigns supreme.

Long-Distance Migration

Although I shall discuss the subject of migration in more detail in a later section, it definitely merits mention here, since it is one of the most intriguing attributes of this family of birds. Of the 25 species of hummingbirds that have been recorded in North America north of the Mexican border, 14 are classified as regular breeders. The other 11 species occur irregularly and do not breed here. Of the 14 regulars, the Rufous Hummingbird *(Selasphorus rufus)* may be the champion of long-distance migration. The northernmost breeder of the group, it nests as far north as southern Alaska. Every fall the rufous flies about 2,500 miles from Alaska to Central America, following an inland route that takes it over the Rocky Mountains. This is much farther than swans and pelicans migrate. Sometimes the rufous gets off course and can end up as far east as Nova Scotia or the tip of Florida. On its northward migration in the spring the route is almost exclusively along the Pacific Coast.

The Ruby-throated Hummingbird may be neck and neck with the rufous in terms of long-distance migration. It is thought that the individuals that nest in the central United States and Canada migrate southward and northward straight through Texas and overland in Mexico and Central America. The ones that breed in the eastern United States and the South along the Gulf of Mexico, however, migrate straight over the gulf, a distance of between 500 and 600 miles of open water, depending on the bird's point of departure. More on this later.

"They sneer at gravity, laugh at physics,
and humble the colors of the rainbow."

Pete Dunne, bird writer extraordinaire

THREE

Our Ruby-throated Hummingbird

So far as we know, the earliest published description of the Ruby-throated Hummingbird was a report in 1671 in the *Philosophical Transactions* of Great Britain, which appeared with these words by the Honorable John Winthrop, governor of Connecticut: "'Tis an exceeding little Bird, and only seen in Summer, and mostly in Gardens, flying from flower to flower, sucking Honey out of the flowers as a Bee doth; as it flieth not lighting on the flower, but hovering over it, sucking with its long Bill a sweet substance."

The rubythroat is the only hummingbird seen with any regularity in the East, and it is the only one known to nest east of the Mississippi River. However, there have been rare sightings of several other hummers in the East. For example, in Louisiana alone, eight species of hummingbirds other than the rubythroat have been recorded: Broad-billed, Buff-bellied, Black-chinned, Anna's, Calliope, Broad-tailed, Rufous, and Allen's.

Description

Someone once described a hummingbird as a tiny airborne object that seems to defy the common-sense rules of design. Others have called them frenetic fliers and perpetual-motion fliers. The Ruby-throated Hummingbird fits all those descriptions. It is the smallest bird of eastern North America, and yet it executes one of the lengthiest migrations among hummingbirds. It averages 3 to 4 inches in length from tip of bill to tip of tail. The male is about 25 percent smaller than the female.

Bill Hilton is an ornithologist who specializes in the study of the Ruby-throated Hummingbird in South Carolina. He gives these measurements from his records of rubythroats he has banded on his farm: "Most adult male Ruby-throated Hummingbirds have bills 15 to 18 mm long, and their wing chord— a standard measure of their folded wing from the 'wrist' to the tip of the longest wing feather—is usually 37 mm to 40 mm. By comparison, adult females have bills 17 mm to 21 mm in length, and their wing chord is between 41 mm and 47 mm. These variations may seem small, but they can equal a 25 percent difference in size."

As for weight, Hilton notes that the average adult male weighs between 2.5 and 3.5 grams (adult females 3.5 to 4.5 grams). In other words, he laughingly says, a male rubythroat weighs about the same as two and a half paper clips, or a nickel weighs a little less than two male rubythroats.

It is hard to imagine how so much action and energy can be packed into so tiny a body. People have been pondering this phenomenon of nature for centuries. In 1782 Hector St. John de Crèvecoeur, in his *Letters from an American Farmer*, wondered, "Where do passions find room in so diminutive a body?"

ADULT MALE

The average adult male rubythroat measures 3.75 inches in length and weighs 0.11 ounce. His wingspan is about 5 inches. He has bright metallic emerald-green plumage on the crown (cap), nape, and back. The cap extends through the eye. There is a very small postocular (behind the eye) white spot. The iris is dark brown or black. The chin, cheeks, and ear coverts (feathers that cover the ear slits) are dull black. The rapierlike bill is black and is about the same length as the head is wide, from base of bill to back of head. In some individuals the bill is about 1.33 times the width of the head.

At first glance the gorget (throat) appears to be black, but when seen in the right light or at the right angle, the black is transformed to iridescent ruby red. It can vary from golden to scarlet, depending on the angle at which light strikes it. Once I held a dying rubythroat in my hands, and its gorget reflected what appeared to be pure gold in the sunlight. The male has a broad white forecollar below the gorget.

The male's underparts are grayish white. The sides and flanks are dull gray overlaid with metallic bronzy green or olive. The middle of the breast is darker gray, and the middle of the abdomen is dull white. Imagine that he is wearing a metallic olive-green vest that doesn't quite meet in the middle.

The two central tail feathers are bright emerald green, just like the back. The eight outer tail feathers are dull black. The two central feathers are a good bit shorter than the outer feathers, giving the tail a notched shape. The undertail coverts (crissum) are pale brownish gray, sometimes glossed with green and margined with dull white.

The wings are dusky with bronzy green coverts (feathers at the top of the wing). When at rest the wing tips reach a little past the base of the rectrices (the main tail feathers). The legs and feet are dark brown or dull black and the tiny claws are black.

ADULT FEMALE

The adult female's crown, nape, and back are the same as the male's, glittering emerald green, sometimes shading to yellowish green or golden green. Her forehead is a little duller than his. Her bill is black and slightly longer than her head from base of bill to back of head. Her eyes are black. She, too, has a very small white spot behind the eyes. Her cheeks are dull grayish white, and her wings are dusky like the male's.

Her throat is white and usually unmarked, though in some females there are obscure dusky speckles on the throat. She has a broad whitish forecollar that extends as squarish patches on the sides of her neck. Her underparts (throat, breast, and belly) are buffy white with a brownish to cinnamon wash on the sides. Her flanks and undertail coverts are usually more or less tinged with a pale buffy brownish color.

The two middle tail feathers are the same color as the back. The remainder of the rectrices are broader and less sharply pointed than in the male, with the three outermost tail feathers being metallic bronzy green on the basal portions, brownish black for the subterminal third, and broadly tipped with white. The fourth tail feathers from the center are longer than the central and outer feathers. This makes the tail appear to be rounded on each side, as opposed to the notched tail of the male. Her legs and feet are black.

Some immature males begin to show red speckles on the throat by early fall. Photograph by Curtis E. Williams.

At first glance, the gorget (throat) of the adult male appears to be black. Photograph by Curtis E. Williams.

IMMATURE MALE

The immature male rubythroat resembles the adult female, right down to the white spots on the three outer tail feathers. His underparts are usually a little more tinged with buffy brown than hers, especially on the sides and flanks. The feathers of his upper parts are very narrowly and obscurely margined with pale gray, light brown, or pale buff. His bill is almost always a bit shorter than the adult's.

At first his throat is white like the adult female's, but the older he gets, the more streaks and ruby speckles will become visible on his neck. Some immature males begin to show these spots by early fall, but no great progress is made in this direction before they head south in migration. In late summer I have seen some young males that looked as if they were wearing ruby necklaces, with brilliant tiny iridescent feathers dotting the throat on thin dusky lines. Their full adult plumage is assumed before they return north in the spring.

IMMATURE FEMALE

The immature female rubythroat closely resembles the adult female, except the throat may show varying amounts of greenish or dusky streaking or spotting. Female Ruby-throated Hummingbirds never show any trace of ruby red on the throat at any age. The young female's lower parts may be more buffy than the adult female's, and her sides and flanks are usually less metallic green.

It is difficult to distinguish an immature female from an adult female; however, the gape (inside mouth lining) is usually a bright yellow or orange in the immature and provides a distinctive identifying characteristic if you see one with its mouth open.

Similar Species

BLACK-CHINNED HUMMINGBIRD

There are some species that may be misidentified as the Ruby-throated Hummingbird. Near the western limit of its breeding range, the rubythroat overlaps with the Black-chinned Hummingbird, and the two may well be confused. At first glance the males look like identical twins. On closer inspection, however, the gorget of the blackchin reflects deep purple or violet where the rubythroat's reflects red. The bill of the blackchin is visibly longer than the rubythroat's, measuring a good 1.5 times the length of the head. The wings of the blackchin appear to be quite long, with bluntly rounded tips. At rest, the wing tips almost reach the tip of the tail.

The females of the two species present a different problem. At first, to the casual observer, they seem identical, like the males. However, there are some subtle clues to look for that should help you distinguish the two. First of all, remember to check the length of the bill. The rubythroat's is 1 to 1.1 times the length of the head. The blackchin's is about 1.5 times the length of the head. That is a noticeable difference. To me, the bill of the blackchin looks much thinner and more needlelike than that of the rubythroat. If the birds are at rest, check the wing length: do the wing tips almost reach the end of the tail, as in the blackchin; or do they barely reach past the base of the rectrices, as in the rubythroat?

Next, the rubythroat female has mostly white underparts where the blackchin's are more grayish or dirty-looking. The cap of the rubythroat is green, and the blackchin's is brown. The throat of the female rubythroat is mostly white; rarely, it is finely streaked. The blackchin female's throat is always finely streaked. While the hummingbird is feeding, the tail of the blackchin wobbles up and down noticeably, and the rubythroat's does not wobble at all.

BROAD-TAILED HUMMINGBIRD

The western version of the rubythroat is the Broad-tailed Hummingbird *(Selasphorus platycercus)*, a surefire candidate for hummer of the Rocky Mountain and Great Basin ranges of the West. Both males have the red gorget and look quite similar, but the shrill rattle made by the male broadtail's rapidly beating wings is unmistakable. It is one of the most characteristic sounds of summer in these high mountain regions and is a sure giveaway of the species' presence. The rubythroat doesn't even come close to making such a sound. Besides, the nesting ranges of the two species are widely separated, with no overlap whatsoever. Broadtails nest along the eastern edge of California and south from Montana and Idaho along the Rocky Mountains into Mexico. If a vagrant should wander into the other's domain, they can easily be sorted out by tail shape or sound. The tail of the broadtail is long and rounded, and the rubythroat's is shorter and slightly forked in the male. The female broadtail has a lot of rufous (reddish brown) on her underparts, where the rubythroat is mostly white.

SPHINX MOTH

The day-flying hawk moth (or sphinx moth, of the family Sphingidae) could easily be mistaken for a Ruby-throated Hummingbird, since it sometimes feeds from flowers in a fashion similar to that of hummers. The hawk moth has no bill, but it hovers like a hummingbird, probes flowers, and extracts nectar with its long flexible tongue, which it coils back next to its mouth when not in use. The moths are about the same size as rubythroats. One evening a neighbor called to tell me that scores of hummers were swarming around his mimosa tree, which was in full bloom. I went over to investigate. Sure enough, they turned out to be hawk moths instead of hummers.

Distribution

No matter what you choose to call it, the Ruby-throated Hummingbird is the best-known hummingbird in North America because it is the most widely distributed of those that reside in the continental United States and Canada. Its breeding range covers the eastern two-thirds of North America. It reaches from the East Coast to the middle of the Great Plains (North Dakota, Nebraska, Kansas, and Central Texas), and from Canada (central Alberta, rarely, east to Nova Scotia) to the Gulf Coast. The rubythroat is the only hummingbird that holds the distinction of nesting both east and west of the Mississippi River. Though they are rarely seen west of the Great Plains, except in Canada, rubythroats show up in odd places at odd times. For instance, far-west sightings were reported from Crow's Nest Pass, British Columbia, in 1983; and Minot, North Dakota, and Truckee, California, in 1984. How they happened to be in those locations is anybody's guess.

Some Ruby-throated Hummingbirds spend as much as seven or eight months in some parts of their breeding range. They generally arrive in the southern states by mid to late March and don't leave there until September or October. In some of those locations they may linger until some time in November. A few individuals are known to overwinter in southern locales, especially in coastal Texas in and near the Rio Grande delta.

In winter rubythroats sometimes occur casually to the eastern edge of the Edwards Plateau in the Texas Hill Country and as far north as North Carolina and southern Alabama. Consequently, a lot of people have a long time to become acquainted with this tiny Neotropical migrant as it darts from flower to flower in their gardens or sips nectar from hummingbird feeders.

Most rubythroats spend an average of four to five months out of the year on their wintering grounds, from middle Florida, south Texas, and south Louisiana through southern Mexico and the rest of Middle America to Panama (from late October or early November until late March or early April). They occur casually in Cuba, Hispaniola, the Bahama Islands, and Bermuda.

The rubythroat is the smallest bird of eastern North America. It is tame, pugnacious, and dazzling to look at. Those features and the extended period that it remains in our part of the world make it one of the favorites of all garden birds of the eastern United States and Canada, an all-American bird.

Habitats

In what types of habitat might one expect to find the Ruby-throated Hummingbird? During breeding season it is likely to be found in gardens from central Alberta eastward to Nova

Scotia, south to the Gulf Coast and Florida, and west to North Dakota, Nebraska, Kansas, and Central Texas—in short, almost anywhere nectar-rich flowers are found. In simple terms the preferred habitat of rubythroats is forests and gardens. That covers a lot of territory, so let's be a little more specific. In the eastern United States the bird prefers mixed woodlands and deciduous forests that are rich in flowering plants. Sometimes it breeds in city parks or in other areas planted with special hummingbird flowers. Usually, there is a stream or some other source of water nearby, as well as trees and thickets for shelter, perching, and nesting activities.

In Canada the rubythroat is generally associated with woodland clearings and edges, gardens, and orchards. At the western edge of its breeding range, in North Dakota, it prefers brushy margins or openings of tracts of deciduous forest, including river floodplain and upland forests. At its southwestern limits, in Texas, it occurs in open coniferous and mixed woodlands, meadows with scattered groves and flowering vegetation, and urban areas.

On their wintering grounds rubythroats compete with tropical hummingbirds for food sources, often in surroundings very different from their northern breeding grounds. In Costa Rica, rubythroats are found on dry, scrubby hillsides, in orchards, and around haciendas—a far cry from the swamps and woodlands in which they nest back home.

Habitats where hummingbirds are typically not found are seashores (unless they are getting ready to take off from the Gulf of Mexico shore in migration), grasslands, and treeless sage areas of the western Great Plains.

Sounds

Oftentimes we hear hummers before we see them. Perhaps it is a chirp or squeak, or maybe simply the humming sound of the wings. Even though it is a soft, obscure sound, somehow, when we hear it, we know a hummer is near.

Although most birds have fairly large sound-producing

mechanisms in their anatomy, hummingbirds do not. Instead they have two small sets of vocal muscles in the trachea, which render them incapable of producing loud sounds. Most hummers are limited to uttering high-pitched, soft twitterings for the most part.

Still, some species of hummingbirds possess what can be called true song. The tiny Vervain Hummingbird *(Mellisuga minima)* of the West Indies is one of these. It warbles in a weak but sweetly melodious manner for as long as ten minutes at a time. The Wine-throated Hummingbird *(Atthis ellioti)* of Central America is another that sings. It utters a sweetly varied outpouring of sounds that last for almost a minute. The Wedge-tailed Sabrewing *(Campylopterus curvipennis)* of Mexico has a song that is described by Steve Howell as "a loud, prolonged, gurgling warble interspersed with squeaky chipping." Among North American hummers, the Anna's comes closest to having a song, with its elaborate courtship vocalizations.

The sounds of Ruby-throated Hummingbirds have been described as chatters, chips, chirps, clinks, squeaks, squeals, jabberings, hisses, buzzes, drones, tchews, and more. The sounds are high-pitched and sometimes have a petulant quality; some are angry-sounding mouselike squeaks. They are usually delivered in a jerky, excited manner. Often the sounds run into nervous, fretful chatterings, but they are always very sharp and clear, though by no means loud. Roy Bedichek, a Texas naturalist, described mating rubythroats buzzing over a patch of buckeye "with a drone which sounded like a fleet of approaching airplanes."

Generally, a lone hummer is silent except for the humming of its wings. According to Arthur Cleveland Bent, when several birds get together they often become quite voluble and quarrelsome and jerk out their notes, now arranged in emphatic phrases, squealing and chattering back and forth as if they were carrying on an animated conversation.

Perhaps you have observed a single hummer approaching another that is perched near a source of food. The approaching bird threatens the perched hummer with jabbers and squeaks, and they begin to dart after one another in flight. After much whirling and jousting about in the air, the winner returns quietly to the food source and the loser departs. Their notes are usually in patterns of twos, threes, or more, and the pitch may run upward or downward. The last note of a series is usually sharply accented.

However soft or frenzied these sounds may be, they serve the same functions as song for warblers, vireos, and other songbirds. It may be said that rubythroats and many other hummers use a form of sign language or body language to convey messages to the opposite sex or to an enemy more than they use sound. In other words, in place of singing, they dance. Diane Ackerman, naturalist and poet, put it this way: "If they can't serenade a mate, or yell war cries at a rival, how can they perform the essential dramas of their lives? They dance. Using body language, they spell out their intentions and moods, just as bees, fireflies, or hula dancers do." Ackerman aptly describes hummers as "mute dancers."

So it is not always necessary to use loud vocalizations to get the message across. The male Ruby-throated Hummingbird performs his share of elaborate aerial ballets in which he twirls, jousts, sideswipes, and somersaults without uttering much sound at all. When we are fortunate to be close enough to a hummer that is feeding, we may hear soft chips or chirps as it sips nectar from flowers or feeders in our gardens, and almost always we hear the soft humming of its gossamer wings.

Threats to Survival

Hummingbirds so charmed Europeans and Americans that people almost loved them to death. In the nineteenth century, stuffed hummingbirds, as well as other birds, became a popular item for use as decorations on women's hats, gowns, and jewelry—not just a feather or two, but whole birds. They were so much in demand during this period that as many as 400,000 skins a year were imported by one London dealer alone, and dealers in Paris and New York were equally as active in this bizarre trade. The plume trade became big business. It was vast, well organized, and well financed.

Besides the trade in skins as fashion adornments, naturalist collectors and museums bought sought-after prize specimens as well. There are six species of hummingbirds in museums today that are known only by these trade skins: two from Brazil, three from Colombia, and one from Bolivia. No one knows if these six are actually now extinct or whether they were simply hybrids and not true species. The fact remains that humans are a detriment to birdlife when we become too enamored of a species or a family of birds.

After 1908 the National Association of Audubon Societies launched a widespread publicity campaign against plume hunters. Finally, in 1910, the Audubon Plumage Bill was pushed through the New York state legislature, banning the sale of wild-bird plumage anywhere in the state. This included New York City, the center of America's millinery trade. In 1913 the federal government got into the act, with a reinforcing law that barred the importation of wild-bird plumage of any sort into the United States. Other states soon followed their lead, and the fight was on to save the birds.

Even though that type of trade is outlawed, unfortunately other human activities are still the main threat to birds on both sides of the Mexican border: the destruction of forests and the replacement of other natural vegetation by crops and housing and commercial developments. Returning rubythroats must be dumbfounded when they look for and don't find the woodlands or parks in which they nested the previous year. Rubythroats winter from southern Mexico into Panama. In some parts of their winter range, habitat destruction has been rampant for years. Somehow, rubythroats have found a way to survive near the plantations that have taken the place of forests, but few hummers find food where forests have been replaced by cattle pastures and row crops such as cotton.

"I send you withal a little Box, with A Curiosity in it . . .
a curiously contrived Nest of a Humming Bird, so called
from the humming noise it maketh whilst it flies. . . . There
are in the same Nest two of that Birds eggs. Whether they
use to have more at once, I know not."

John Winthrop, governor of Connecticut
Philosophical Transactions (Great Britain), 1671

"They breed in little Nests made up like a bottom of
Silk-like matter, their eggs no bigger than white Pease."

John Josselyn of Scarborough, Maine
New-Englands Rarities, 1672

FOUR

Courtship and Life
around the Nest

*T*hrough the centuries hundreds of ornithologists and bird-watchers have discovered hummingbirds in the process of building their nests. French colonists mentioned them as early as 1558. But for me, the unforgettable experience happened fifteen years ago on a spring day in Texas.

> *Wednesday, April 21, 1982, Waco, Texas. Partly cloudy with intermittent light rain. Temperature, upper 50s to low 60s. While birding with Audubon group in Cameron Park, found a female hummer building her nest. Saw a male rubythroat feeding nearby; surmised he was her mate.*

When I spotted her, the female rubythroat was in a frenzy. She flitted away and back again and again to the same spot on the limb of a pecan tree that was next to the main thoroughfare in Waco's largest city park. Her persistence in returning to the same location piqued my curiosity. I focused my binoculars on the scant beginnings of what eventually would become an intricate work of art—a small lichen-covered platform saddling the crook of a slender downsloped branch. There are records of rubythroat nests from 4 to 50 feet above the ground, with the average height being between 10 and 20 feet. This nest was 2 feet from the outer extremity of the limb and about 20 feet above the ground.

The ideal nesting site for a Ruby-throated Hummingbird requires four things: (1) a small downsloped branch for better drainage during rain (sometimes the branch is covered with lichens), (2) umbrellalike protection overhead, (3) a water supply, and (4) a source of food nearby. This hummer had found all four. I have already described the branch. Her umbrella was near perfection. The thickly clustered leaves on the limb above the nest site provided ample protection from sun and rain. The chosen tree was a few feet from a spring-fed creek with an abundant supply of wild honeysuckle, Turk's cap, and trumpet vine on its banks.

While the female worked, I set up my spotting scope a safe distance away, and presto! I had a ringside seat at one of nature's unfolding dramas. Since the female hummingbird does all the work in building the nest, incubating the eggs, and feeding the young, I didn't expect to see the male. Several times while I was watching the nest I did see a male Ruby-throated Hummingbird feeding in the vicinity, but I could never be sure he was her mate. Hummingbirds are typically loners and bond with the opposite sex for only the few seconds it takes to mate.

Peering through my scope, I watched the female make repeated trips to the surrounding area. With her tiny bill, she gathered small pieces of plant fiber, plant down, and spider silk to weave into the nest. Periodically, this dainty atom of birdlife visited one of the many tent caterpillar nests that are abundant in the park during spring and summer. She was careful not to become entangled in the netlike tent as she stole strands of the web, and she rushed back to the building site with the treasure gripped in her bill. She then sat on the unfinished rim of the nest, facing outward. She bent double, lowered her head, and deftly draped the strips around the outer perimeter to bind together the down and fiber. In the same fashion she anchored the structure by wrapping spider's silk around the nest and the branch, as though tying a gaily wrapped package with the finest of silk ribbons.

To make the center of the nest soft enough to protect eggs and young, she plucked from the air bits of fluff (seeds) that were drifting down from the many cottonwood trees in the park. She stuffed each airy tuft into the inner part of the nest. First she poked it with her bill, then she stomped it into place with her feet. Finally she sat on the downy seat, wiggled herself about as if on a swivel, and thus molded the soft lining to fit her body. She repeated this process with every piece of down that she collected, and it took hundreds of trips to fill the minute cup.

Saturday, April 24, 10:00 A.M. 55 °F. Though it is raining, she is still working.

When I arrived that day it looked as if the nest was almost complete. Once she had built the rim to the desired height, she carefully extracted bits of lichen from nearby trees to decorate the outside walls, a task that must have required enormous stamina. I examined a similar Ruby-throated Hummingbird nest from a study collection in Baylor University's biology department. It was about the size of a silver dollar. It easily fit into my smallest demitasse (1.75 by 1.75 inches) with room to spare. On the outside of the study specimen I counted more than 200 fragments of lichens. Keep in mind that every individual piece must be extracted from the tree trunk with her bill, carried to the building site, and stuck in place by the magical glue hummingbirds manufacture from their saliva. Imagine a human transporting every single brick from a great distance on foot to her own home building site, and mortaring it into place with the greatest of care, using some magical solution extracted from the human body.

Monday, April 26, 9:00–10:30 A.M. Female sitting on nest.
She leaves every few minutes but soon returns. She sits low in
nest so I can see only her head and tail above the nest rim.

The length of time required for building the nest seems highly variable. I don't know how long the female had been working on this nest when I discovered her. Judging from the progress made on that first day, I would guess it was two to three days. Hummingbird nests are sometimes built in one day, but usually it takes one to ten days. As I looked at this tiny piece of art—a masterpiece of design and construction—I wondered how anyone, bird or human, could create such a complex dwelling in ten days, much less in only one day. In a Maya legend, birds who asked a tribal wise man how to build a sturdy nest were sent to the hummingbirds for lessons. Certainly, humans could benefit from the same advice for building a sturdy structure. Hummingbirds are undoubtedly among the most accomplished of avian architects.

Five days after I discovered the beginnings of this structure, the female was sitting on the nest as if incubating eggs. The activity of nest-building increases the female's readiness to mate, and she seeks out a male on his feeding territory when her nest is almost complete. She lets him know she is ready and willing to mate by *not* fleeing when he approaches her in an aggressive manner. One of my biggest regrets about this whole experience is that I was not there to observe the beautiful aerobatic courtship ballet, an integral part of the breeding ritual of Ruby-throated Hummingbirds.

When the male sees the female sitting quietly on her perch, he begins one of his spectacular displays. He may perform something called pendulum-arc flight, at which time he flies back and forth, in front of the female, on the precise path of a wide arc. It almost looks as if the male is held up by an invisible swinging wire. Connie Toops describes it as "swaying broadly like a pocket watch dangling from a chain." He may rise on either side of the arc to a height of 3 to 40 feet. At the lowest point in the arc the male frequently passes close to the head of the female and makes a loud buzzing sound, probably the result of the motion of his wings and tail.

The sun shimmering from his gorget reflects light like a flashing red neon sign. To a human observer the female may seem uninterested during this impressive aerobatic display. If indeed she is interested in this particular male, after he finishes his pendulum-arc flight, she streaks away to some distance from his territory, he follows her, and there copulation takes place. The male mounts the back of the female and clings there, half perched and half hovering, and cloacal contact is made for approximately two seconds. Afterward, the female preens and goes about her nest-building activities. He returns to his territory.

A second possible visual display that may occur between the prospective mates is called vertical flight. In this display the male and the female fly vertically up and down while facing each other about one to two feet apart, all the while twittering at each other. Or they may fly upward in a spiraling pattern. One report indicated that after such behavior the birds were observed copulating on the ground.

There is one other display, called horizontal flight, that may be seen. Some writers think it is part of aggressive encounters between hummingbirds or between hummingbirds and other species of birds, and some think it is courtship behavior. In horizontal flight, one bird sits on a perch while the other flies back and forth along a short horizontal path. Some say a chase ensues after the horizontal flight, and then copulation occurs.

During all the visual displays just described, both sexes fly with their tails spread wide in fanlike fashion. After the female is fertilized the male goes back to his own feeding territory of about one-fourth of an acre and resumes his normal activities, which may include copulating with one or numerous other females.

After mating, the female preens and then returns to her almost completed nest to lay her eggs. Although during the birds' brief mating tryst, millions of sperm are deposited through her cloaca, they swim up her oviduct to fertilize just two ova. Almost invariably Ruby-throated Hummingbirds lay two diminutive, elliptical, white, unmarked eggs. Such a tiny nest could hardly hold more than two. The eggs are usually laid early in the morning, with an interval of one to two days between layings. Arthur Cleveland Bent, in his 1940 work, reported no exceptions to the rule of two eggs, but W. A. Welter reported in 1935 that in one nest he observed, there was only one egg.

The average size of eggs is 13.0 by 8.4 millimeters, about the size of a black-eyed pea or a small bean. Each weighs about 0.02 ounce. The female hummer weighs about 8 times her egg weight; the female Ostrich, the world's largest bird, is 60 times the weight of her egg.

It seems that the dates hummingbird eggs are laid vary according to the location. Egg dates in Texas are as early as April 14 and as late as June 22, according to Harry C. Oberholser. Paul A. Johnsgard dates egg-laying from late March to June 15 in Florida, from late May to early July in New York, and from June 1 to July 17 in Michigan.

The female may start laying eggs before the nest is completed, and some authorities say she begins incubation after the first egg is laid. She may spend 60 to 80 percent of the day incubating the eggs; it depends on the weather. Naturally, on cooler days, more time is required to keep the eggs at a constant temperature. In hot weather the female may spend most of her time simply protecting the eggs from the heat of the sun by spreading her wings, umbrella fashion, to shade them. Although Bent reports some shorter incubation periods, the normal time is probably sixteen days. The female may continue to add bits of lichen and soft nest-lining materials throughout the incubation period. Sometimes it may be added even up to two weeks after the nestlings have hatched.

Some females have more than one brood. Some have as many as three broods. There are some records of a female rubythroat starting a second brood while still attending the first brood. Donald and Lillian Stokes note that there is a record of one female Ruby-throated Hummingbird tending two nests at the same time. The nests were on the same limb of the tree, and only 3.5 feet apart. The little female kept busy feeding the almost full-sized young in the first nest while incubating two eggs in the second nest. The Stokeses reported that all three nestlings fledged successfully.

If for some reason there is a nesting failure (for instance, if a predator steals the eggs, or if a storm destroys the nest limb), most females will attempt to nest again. If the nest is still intact she will use it again, refurbishing it as necessary. If not, she begins again from scratch.

Wednesday, May 12, 8:45 A.M. Cloudy with scattered showers. Hummer sitting higher in nest. I can see her back as well as head and tail. She seemed nervous when wind came up. Branch with nest bobbing up and down. At 12:15 P.M. she is still sitting.

For the next two and a half weeks I returned to the nest in Cameron Park with almost as much regularity as the hummer did. Soon I was on speaking terms with all the park personnel. During this period my notes indicate that each time I was there the female was patiently sitting. She left the nest only long

A female sits on her nest in the rain.
Photograph by Beth K. Hawkins.

enough to attend to her own bodily needs, which is about what I was doing as well.

I also noted that the female often turned herself around to face a new direction in the nest. Each time she did this she rearranged the lichens where her chin rested on the rim of the nest. She reminded me of myself, fluffing my pillow each time I turn over in bed at night.

Thursday, May 13, 8:00 A.M. Raining and 63 °F. Hummer sitting low in nest and very still.

In the wee hours of the morning I was awakened by the noisy intensity and furor of a spring thunderstorm with high winds, heavy rain, and rolling thunder. My first thought was of the hummer. Could she possibly survive the hard downpour and gusty wind? I could hardly wait for daybreak so I could go and check on her.

I needn't have worried. When I arrived at the park, she was snug and dry. She sat low in the nest and rocked gently with each gust of wind, like the figurehead of a ship that bounds up and down with every wave. Her wings were spread like a tent and covered the entire opening of the nest. Once she rose up and poked about inside the nest with her bill. I wondered if she was turning the eggs, or if she might be attending nestlings.

"Have the babies arrived?" I wondered. Seventeen days had elapsed since she began sitting on the nest, and incubation usually requires sixteen days. According to my calculations, the chicks should have hatched on May 12 or 13. When hummingbird chicks are ready to make their debut into the world, they use a sharp appendage on the beak called an egg tooth to break out of the eggshell. This special tool falls off soon after hatching.

Sunday, May 16, 5:00 P.M. Mother hummer sitting high on nest. She left momentarily and visited honeysuckle. Returned and sat on rim of nest. Made motions indicating she was feeding two babies. Oh, for a telephone lineman's hydraulic lift so I could sneak a peek inside that nest!

Although I couldn't see them from my vantage point, I was now almost certain there were two nestlings. When newly hatched, a hummingbird is about the size of a wasp. Consequently, I concluded, two babies could easily be concealed in the depths of this tiny receptacle.

Hummingbird nestlings are altricial—nearly naked, blind, and helpless when first born. Alexander Skutch describes them as "ugly, uncompromising little grubs." They have slate-blue skin, tightly drawn over diminutive skeletons, and a line of yellowish down along their backs. Right after hatching, their bills are short, wide, and yellow and don't really look like hummingbird bills at all, but rather more like bumps.

The first meal the nestlings receive from their mother is a nutritious broth of nectar and tiny insects. For the first few days their meals fill their crops till they bulge—they almost look as if there are tumors on their necks.

Since the young don't develop down feathers to keep them warm, the mother must brood them to help regulate their body temperature. Even though young hummingbirds may seem delicate, they are remarkably tough. From the time they are about twelve days old, they are able to maintain their own body temperature inside their snug little nest, and the female no longer has to brood them. When the hatchlings are only a few days old, they develop a set of pin feathers, which is the plumage they wear until after fledging (leaving the nest).

Monday, May 17, 12:00–12:30 P.M. Rained all morning but stopped by noon. This time I didn't worry about her.

When I arrived at the park today, the mother hummer was sitting high on the nest. I could see one tiny gaping yellow mouth as she reached down with her bill to feed the nestlings. Young hummingbirds must be fed frequently on a high-protein and high-energy diet. Consequently, the mother must find plenty of insects as well as nectar to nourish her young. This nest site had an abundant nectar supply composed of Turk's cap, trumpet vines, and honeysuckle on the banks of the creek nearby.

A female sits at the side of her nest.
Photograph by Beth K. Hawkins.

The female probably found an adequate supply of insects there as well.

The nest's location near a busy street seemed of no concern to the mother. Neither was she disturbed when on several occasions I took groups of people to see the nest. I was always careful to maintain a discreet distance between us and the nest tree. The only thing that seemed to bother her was when joggers bounced along the trail directly beneath the nest limb. Though the joggers were oblivious to her presence, they regarded me rather quizzically, clearly wondering why that woman was peering through a scope at the limb of a pecan tree. When the joggers came by, the female hummer always stretched her neck as tall as she possibly could and peered down at them until they were out of her line of vision. It was almost as if she were expressing her disapproval.

Once a squirrel ventured too close for her comfort. Even though he was 20 feet away and in a different tree, she flew at him threateningly and informed him clearly that this was her domain. Imagine! Such a tiny creature attempting to intimidate an animal many times her own size! Hummingbirds have been known to chase creatures of various sizes, from bumblebees competing for feeding rights to flowers, to eagles seen flying over their territory.

Twice while I was watching, a Barred Owl swooped across the open space near her homestead, but the female remained calm. I was more worried than she seemed to be. I suppose she knew she was much too small a nibble to satisfy the owl's gigantic appetite. Besides, her nest, covered with lichen and plant fiber, looked like a knot on the limb. It could easily be missed even by a keen-eyed hunter such as a Barred Owl.

Friday, May 21, 12:00 NOON. The mother is gone. No sign of babies. Must be nap time. Lots of traffic and noise in the park. There's a big high school gathering at a picnic shelter nearby.

Fifteen minutes after I arrived amid all the chaos, the mother appeared unperturbed by the jubilant yelling of 200 teenagers.

She calmly went on with the care and feeding of her own two preteens. This was the first time I was certain there were two nestlings.

Approximately every fifteen minutes now, the busy little female comes to feed her offspring. Typically, she sits on the rim of the nest and braces her tail against its side before plunging her bill into theirs. The sound of the mother's wings and the air brushing across their developing feathers stimulates the young birds to gape (open their mouths wide). Bob Sargent, hummingbird bander from Alabama, says he can hum near the nest and get the same response. Brightly colored mouth linings of red or yellow provide highly visible targets for the female even in the shade of the nest.

It is a mystery to me how a mother hummingbird avoids piercing the delicate lining of those tiny throats as she jabs her rapierlike bill straight down into their gaping mouths and pumps the regurgitated food (nectar and insects) from her crop into theirs. This is just one of the many astounding feats these creatures perform. Even though her bill is sharp, fortunately, so is her aim.

As the young grow larger and their bills are longer, the mother may place her bill into theirs at a right angle instead of straight in. Even later, the food may be passed directly from her beak into theirs.

A mother hummingbird makes anywhere from 20 to 60 trips a day to collect nectar for her young. She may also catch as many as 2,000 insects a day, since her nestlings require a high-energy diet that is rich in nectar *and* insects. After about four trips to feed the young, the female makes one trip to feed herself. Her nesting duties make a huge demand on her energy supply, so she, too, must eat often to keep up her strength.

After feeding the nestlings, the mother sits on the side of the nest and waits for the babies to defecate. With her bill, she then removes from the nest a fecal sac that contains the feces. It looks like a small white plastic package. She carries the sac far away from the nest site to avoid attracting predators. For the first few days after the babies are hatched, their digestive tracts are not highly developed. Consequently, as a matter of food economy, the mother sometimes eats the fecal sacs until her offspring are a little older.

Saturday, May 22, 9:15 A.M. Two bills showing!

By now the bills have grown in length at a rapid rate and are not stubby and yellow anymore. Now they are relatively long and dark, and the nestlings are bright-eyed and alert. I observe that one baby has learned to reach for protein by darting its threadlike tongue in and out to catch tiny insects that are flitting about the nest. While this one showed off its newfound insect-catching ability, the other backed itself to the edge of the nest, raised up, and expelled feces over the nest rim. This seems very accommodating, for now the mother will no longer have to clean house every time one of the babies defecates.

Tuesday, May 25. Took my bird class to see nest. Babies visible as they move around. Mama buzzing in and out. Didn't feed them while we were watching. Intervals between feedings growing longer.

During the week of this journal entry, I taught a class on birding in Baylor University's Summer School for Retired Persons. Naturally, I was eager to share with the class this drama in nature that I had watched so closely over a month. On one of the field trips I took the group to the park to see the hummers. Each of the senior citizens took a turn to look through the spotting scope. The nestlings cooperated beautifully. Everyone saw the miniature heads with bulging eyes and daggerlike bills. Occasionally a diminutive brown wing was visible as a baby stretched and turned. By now the babies have learned to preen their pin feathers with their feet and bills. Too, they have become adventurous enough to explore nearby vegetation with their tongues.

One of the handy features of a hummingbird nest is that it is constructed in such a way that it is flexible enough to expand as the babies grow larger and begin to move around. We imagined that we could see the sides of the nest pulsating with each turn of the babies and every stretch of their wings. In truth, it probably was not a figment of our imagination at all. Today the mother kept her distance. She perched on a small twig where she could see both the nest and us at all times. She buzzed by twice, hovered a few inches above the nest, communicated some twitterings to the nestlings, and was off again.

As we started back to the van, one man in the class commented that this was a first for his seventy-five years. I thought I saw the hint of a tear in his twinkling eyes as he thanked me for showing him the nest.

Wednesday, May 26, 11:30 A.M. Stopped to see nest on my way home from class. Mama was feeding her young. Why couldn't she have done it for my class yesterday? Only one small head and bill visible. Two large flies crawling on side of nest. Has one baby died?

I worried all the way home. Somehow I felt responsible for this little family. I was glad to have an excuse to go back to the nest when Barbara Garland, a good friend and photographer, called after lunch and asked if I had time to go with her to the park. She had tried unsuccessfully several times to get pictures of the mother feeding the babies. She wanted to try one more time.

When we reached the pecan tree a few minutes after Barbara's call, we saw the mother perched on a nearby lookout. We could see only one wobbly head poking out of the nest, and the flies were still crawling around the rim. It appeared certain now that something had happened to one of the nestlings. We searched the ground directly beneath the nest and found no evidence of remains. Either the nestling had died of natural causes or it was the victim of a predator. All we know is that from that point on we saw only one baby in the nest.

Barbara set up her camera and tripod, focused the lens on the surviving nestling, and we waited for the mother to return.

In 45 minutes she arrived with a throat full of nectar. It took only a few seconds for each feeding, so Barbara quickly snapped a series of exposures.

A few days before fledging, nestlings may be seen sitting on the rim of the nest exercising their wings. This exercise is important for developing their young muscles. They anchor themselves to the nest rim and rapidly vibrate their wings in preparation for their first flight, which may be no farther than 50 feet. From the outset, they are expert fliers. Indeed, they may be seen hovering, backing, and darting about with almost as much dexterity as their parents. Landing, on the other hand, may be a different matter for the fledgling. At first they have trouble figuring out how to land safely and perch with those tiny feet nature has provided them. As in almost any endeavor, practice makes perfect, and soon they are adept at flying and landing.

All along I had hoped to be present for this special flight event. Unfortunately, Memorial Day weekend came at just the wrong time in the hummers' schedule. According to my calculations, Saturday, May 29, should be the sixteenth day after hatching—flying day for the little hummer.

Long before my discovery of the hummer's nest, our family had planned a birding trip for that weekend to Bolivar Peninsula on the upper Texas coast. Reluctantly, I took up my scope, left the hummers, and drove to the coast. Although my eyes focused on the plethora of shorebirds that are ever-present at Bolivar, my thoughts remained focused on a walnut-sized knot on the limb of a pecan tree back home in Waco.

Sunday, May 30. Port Bolivar, Texas. Seventeenth day after hatching. Decided to leave our vacation spot one day early on the outside chance of catching a glimpse of the surviving nestling before it fledged and was gone.

We arrived back in Waco around 5 P.M. Recognizing my feelings of anxiety, my husband suggested that we drive to the park before going home. When we reached the nesting site, I got out of the car quickly and set up the scope. There was the baby, sitting on the side of the nest exercising its wings. With its tiny feet clinging tightly to the nest rim, it fluttered its wings as fast as it could. As it turned out, this was my final farewell to the feathered midget. At the time, I didn't know that fledging usually occurs early in the morning, so I arrived at the nest too late the next day to observe the special event. For several days after that, I returned to the park only to find an empty nest.

Although after fledging they never return to the nest to live, fledglings usually stay in the vicinity for several days, and the female continues to feed them for about three weeks. After that the mother begins to behave aggressively toward her offspring. It is thought that the mother now views her offspring as competitors for food, and she attempts to chase them away from her territory. It's hard to imagine that a tiny hummingbird, little more than one month old, is ready to strike out on its own in the world of wildlings, but that is the way of nature.

I never saw this family again. That's easy to understand, since the fledgling period is a time for the young to explore different flowers in their surrounding territory and discover which ones are rich in nectar. It is also a time when the mother may take the young to a hummingbird feeder, if there is one close by, and teach her offspring to drink from an artificial source.

Once my family was privileged to watch as a mother hummingbird brought her two young fledglings to one of our feeders. First the mother fed herself while the babies looked on. Then, while the mother hovered nearby, the youngsters took turns coming to the feeder to try their luck. Each one started at the top of the feeder and slowly made its way down, poking with its bill here and there, until finally it found the source of the sugar water. Soon they were experts at sipping nectar, and we saw them every day until it was time for them to move on in migration.

According to some hummingbird authorities, if the female survives, she may return to the same tree to nest the following year. She may even use the same nest, making necessary repairs, if the nest is still there. You may be sure, the next year I searched the area for that little Ruby-throated Hummingbird. Although her original nest had long since disappeared, I found another active nest less than 100 yards from the one the previous year. It was approximately 30 to 40 feet off the ground in a large oak tree. Of course, I could never be sure that it was the same bird nesting there.

"Feasting, flying, courting and dueling,
hummingbirds consume life at a fever pitch."

Diane Ackerman, "Mute Dancers"

FIVE

Life in the Fast Lane: A Day in the Life of a Male Rubythroat

Now that we have seen what a demanding life a female Ruby-throated Hummingbird leads, particularly during the nesting season, you may wonder how the male passes the time after his short-lived courtship and mating duties are ended.

Remember the old television show *Queen for a Day*? If you had the chance to be a Ruby-throated Hummingbird for a day, would you do it? If so, where would you sleep? What would you eat? How would you bathe and maintain your feathers? Where would you find enough nourishment to sustain you through the day and night? How would you keep other birds from taking over your food source?

Of course, we all know it is impossible to become a hummingbird for a day. Even if invited just to follow one for 24 hours, we couldn't do it; they fly at such a frenetic pace that we simply could not keep up. So let's imagine for a while that we can follow a hummer and see what a typical day is like in the life of a male Ruby-throated Hummingbird in Central Texas after breeding season is over.

Let's begin in early morning. The sun has not yet peeped over the horizon and the air is still cool. The little hummer wakes from a long night spent in the shelter of an evergreen. Since the ambient temperature was lower than his body temperature, he went into a state of suspended animation, called torpor, for those hours of darkness in order to survive the night. Now he must warm up to at least 86°F before he can function normally. Even though his eyes are open, he is not yet able to leave his perch. He must remain there until his rate of metabolism rises with the morning light.

After a few minutes of sitting there motionless, the first thing he does is arch his neck to get the kinks out. Then he flicks his tongue out and in a few times to get rid of the morning blahs. Now he is ready to begin his morning calisthenics. He shakes his wings one at a time and flaps his tail. Slowly, he opens his wings fully and stretches them alongside his body, just as humans stretch their arms and yawn upon getting out of bed. The hummer moves his wings back and forth and side to side and fans his tail to limber up.

By now, from his roosting place in the mountain cedar, he can see almost the entire red ball as the sun emerges above the horizon on the other side of the Brazos River. Gradually, the hummer's temperature climbs with the sun until it reaches a normal 102° to 108°F. He starts his motor and tries his wings. Still holding onto his perch with both feet, he flaps his wings at a rate of 50 to 75 times per second. On this day it has been about 30 minutes from the moment he opened his eyes to this point, when his wings are capable of lifting him into orbit. On some mornings it takes as long as an hour, depending on how low the overnight temperature dropped.

Again, he revs his engine. His wings are now beating at a rate of 80 times per second. With wings so powerful, a hummingbird doesn't need to push off from the branch or twig on which it is perched. Our hummer simply rises straight up into the air like a helicopter, entirely on his own power.

Now that he is airborne, the first thing he must do is find nourishment to replenish the energy that was spent sustaining him through the night. He must find nectar and a source of protein—now! Luckily, the territory he claims as his domain, about one-quarter of an acre in a large city park, has a bounteous supply of trumpet creeper vine, Turk's cap, lantana, and wild honeysuckle along a creek bank. From these he extracts nectar for energy, and luckily for him, the insects he requires for protein thrive around these woodland plants. His feeding territory is adjacent to the nesting territory of the female rubythroat in the previous chapter, who could easily have been his mate.

He flits from one blossom to another—six inches away, six feet away—starting and stopping with a jerk. He hovers at each one long enough to insert his bill deep into the throat of the tubular flower until his tongue reaches the elixir he relishes, nectar that accumulated at the base of the blossom overnight.

He chooses long tubular flowers because with them there is less competition from bees and other nectar-eating insects. Just as a cat laps milk, the hummer laps the nectar, at thirteen licks per second, until he has his fill.

His eyes suddenly turn toward the creek that flows through the park. The sun is now part of the way up its climb into the morning sky, and the rubythroat detects a swarm of gnats hovering in a ray of sunlight that dances on the water. Without hesitation, he leaves the flower-lined bank and zooms out over the creek into the middle of the swarming insects. Our high-speed aeronautic wizard flits about in zigzag fashion and hawks the tiny winged creatures much the same as a flycatcher. As he flies through the swarm, his tongue flicks out like a bolt of lightning and snatches an insect from midair faster than the human eye can see. Then his tongue rolls back inside his beak, and he swallows the gnat. Again and again he repeats this action before he returns to the tubular blossoms for more of the sweet stuff.

After a few more minutes of frantic feeding on the energy-giving nectar, it is time to rest and digest his food. He flies like a minihelicopter to his favorite perch, a utility line that runs through the park. From there he commands a view of his entire domain in a wilderness area that has been preserved in the midst of the city. His territory is bounded by Proctor Springs and Sturgis Road on two sides, and University Parks Drive and North Fourth Street on the other two. Spring-fed Wilson Creek bisects his rectangular territory at a 45-degree angle. After alighting on his perch, he cleans his bill by swiping it back and forth across the wire; then he rests and waits for his meal to digest.

In the fast-paced world of hummingbirds, it takes only about five minutes for food to pass from the minute crop into the stomach and less than an hour to convert the nectar into carbohydrate energy. In the contrastingly slower-paced world of humans, the same process requires about nine hours.

Next on his agenda is the care of his feathers, which were ruffled to help keep him warm through the night. No bird

A hummer rises straight up into the air like a helicopter.
Photograph by Luke Wade.

A male moves his head back and forth as if he were watching a tennis game. Photograph by Alan Murphy.

can preen the feathers on its own head or throat with its bill. The longer the bill, the greater the extent of plumage that cannot easily be reached. To solve this problem, many species of birds that are more social than hummingbirds practice something called mutual or social preening. Toucans and ibises, for example, and many other species may be observed preening the feathers on the heads and throats of their mates or other birds. Hummingbirds are loners, however, and do not follow the patterns of the highly social birds in this respect. They have never been seen engaging in social preening after the nestling stage. They can attend to their heads and throats only by scratching.

So it is that our little hummer begins his preening ritual with a scratching session. Carefully, he balances with one foot holding fast to the utility wire. He raises his other foot up and over the top of one wing until it reaches his head. After a thorough head-scratching, he bends his head down so he can reach his throat with his foot and gives it a good scratch. This is called scratch preening. When he is done, he rests with both feet firmly gripping the wire.

Next, he stretches his neck like a contortionist and with his bill touches the oil gland (uropygial gland) at the base of his tail. From this gland he collects oil on his bill for cleaning and waterproofing his feathers. Slowly, he pulls each primary feather of his wings lightly through his beak until all the barbules are realigned. Then he repeats the action with each of the ten feathers in his tail. He uses his claws to preen his wing coverts. To reach his back he contorts his neck once again and fastidiously runs his bill over each feather. Wherever they can be reached, he treats every feather the same way. It is a long and painstaking process, since this midget of a bird has 900 to 1,400 feathers. In proportion to his size, that's a lot of feathers. Some studies show that smaller birds generally have more feathers per unit of body weight than larger birds to help maintain their high internal temperature. Thus he must keep all the feathers properly groomed for maximum efficiency. It is not surprising that larger birds have more feathers than smaller birds. For example, a

Whistling Swan has more than 25,000 feathers and an Eastern Meadowlark has more than 4,600.

It has been more than a quarter of an hour now since he had his first meal of the day. The crop of a hummingbird is tiny, and heat (energy) loss in so small a body is rapid, so he must eat numerous small meals a day rather than a few large meals to replenish his energy. From dawn to sunset, a hummingbird will have, on average, at least 60 meals a day, in order to fulfill its energy requirements. This makes it sound as if a hummingbird does nothing but eat all day. In reality it spends only 10 to 15 percent of its time actually feeding and 75 to 80 percent perched while digesting its food and maintaining its plumage.

Now it is time to feed again. This time he chooses to visit the lantana that is located almost directly beneath his utility-wire perch. It's not unusual for a hummingbird to visit as many as 3,000 blossoms per day to satisfy its appetite. It won't get nectar from every single one of them, but it has to investigate to find which ones have the most nectar. It has been said that curiosity helps hummingbirds survive, for that is the way they find new sources of food. They have been observed investigating all sorts of colorful objects, from red bandannas to red lipstick. Our hummer flies to the garbage can next to the picnic pavilion that is in his territoy. There he examines a red soda can at the top of the heap but finds no reward of nectar.

When the hummer returns to his favorite perch after feeding this time, he sits there and moves his head back and forth almost constantly, as though watching a fast-paced tennis match. He does this to make sure no one is trying to invade his territory. Sure enough, after a few minutes, a Black-chinned Hummingbird approaches from the direction of University Parks Drive and attempts to feed at the Turk's cap near the street. Quick as a flash, our hummer makes a diving pass at the blackchin, and a chase ensues—across the creek, back across University Parks Drive, over the grounds of Cameron Park Zoo, to the Brazos River. It doesn't take long for the interloper to get the message that he is not welcome, and the blackchin departs posthaste. The last time the rubythroat sees the interloper, the blackchin is headed for the residential area east of the river.

After spending so much energy in the chase, the rubythroat goes to the honeysuckle for some refreshment before returning to his guard post to rest. During the chase the hummer used up a lot of oxygen and thus produced excessive heat in his body. Since a hummingbird is so well insulated inside its feathers, it cannot disperse heat through its skin by sweating as humans do. Instead, he has to pant to cool himself. While he is in the process of cooling off in this manner, another intruder zips by. This one is not so easy to vanquish. It is another male rubythroat. The dive and chase doesn't work with him, so our hummer resorts to what is called the dive display. It is similar to the courtship ritual of a male and female rubythroat. The owner of the territory executes a flight path in the shape of a giant ∪. He dives at the intruder from a height of about fifteen feet. With a loud buzzing of the wings when he is nearest the enemy at the bottom of the arc, he rises to a height of fifteen feet again to complete the ∪, and then returns along the same path for several more passes. With his brilliant red gorget flashing in the sun, loud chattering (on the part of both birds), and tail fanned to its full capacity, he continues this display in his attempt to intimidate the intruder, but it doesn't work on this pugnacious invader.

Our determined hummer tries another strategy, which is called vertical flight. The two birds face each other and fly vertically up and down one to two feet apart, all the while chattering in language only a hummingbird can understand. They charge one another like flying missiles, then tumble through the air, striking each other with their feet. They fall to the ground only to rise again. The birds carefully avoid using their beaks as weapons in these frays because they are too important for getting food. Miraculously, neither bird is injured in this fight, although it looks, to the casual observer, as if it could be unto death. Finally, the invading bird has had enough, and he departs.

Again, before going back to his post as sentinel, our hummer, whose energy reserves are just about depleted after the strenuous encounter, investigates the bark of a tree and the undersides of numerous leaves. There he gleans a meal of insects. Only 10 percent of his foraging time is spent finding insects, and the other 90 percent is spent searching for nectar. Although protein from insects is necessary for the bird to live, he gains most of his energy from nectar. So back to the trumpet vine he goes.

A hummingbird has a special relationship with the flowers on which it feeds. The flowers reward the bird with a generous supply of nectar, and the bird in turn acts as pollinator for the flowers. As our hummer probes the tubes of trumpet creeper in the park, pollen dusts his crown, bill, and throat. When he visits other trumpet blossoms, he inadvertently drops some of the pollen on them. This is called cross-pollination, and it is a perfect example of nature in harmony. The process is beneficial to the flowers and to the birds.

By now it is the middle of the afternoon, and a dark cloud suddenly appears in the sky above Cameron Park. A brief summer shower follows, and our little hummer welcomes the respite from the heat of the afternoon. While on his perch, he spreads his feathers and allows the raindrops to penetrate his plumage all the way to the skin. He raises his head skyward, opens his beak, and a few raindrops quench his thirst. After the shower ends, he takes advantage of moisture that is left on the trees and brushes against the leaves to shake the droplets onto his body. Then he shakes all over to get the moisture out and begins his preening ritual all over again.

Throughout the rest of the afternoon, he feeds every fifteen minutes or so, rests, bathes at the shallow edge of the creekbed, preens, and guards against invaders. Since breeding season is over, he has no interest in courting the females in adjoining territories.

Late in the evening, as dusk settles over the park, his feeding frenzy picks up and he fills his crop with enough nectar to sustain him through the night. When it is almost dark, he goes to his favorite roosting place, a skinny branch in a mountain cedar tree. There he settles down in the thick foliage. After a busy day, he is exhausted.

During daylight hours, a hummer has little fear of predators, thanks to unparalleled flying abilities. His high speed allows him to escape harm from most flying predators. Nighttime presents a different problem, for then his body functions are at a low level and he is easy prey for any nocturnal predator looking for a midnight snack. That is why it is essential for him to find a protected place in which to sleep. The mountain cedar provides thick cover for his sleeping chamber.

He can't relax quite yet. For several minutes he scans his territory with side to side movements of his head to make sure no other intruders are about. When he is sure he is safe from harm, his head movements gradually decrease until the bird is motionless. He retracts his neck and draws his head back against his chest. With his head pointing forward and his bill tilted at an upward angle, he is almost ready for sleep.

Since hummingbirds have no down feathers to insulate them from the cold, he fluffs his feathers all over his body for extra warmth, turns down the thermostat, in a manner of speaking, and goes into a zombielike state of torpor to save energy. His body temperature and heart rate are lowered, as are most of his other bodily functions. In such a state his body temperature usually falls nearly to air temperature, and he is able to get through the night by utilizing the food that is stored in his crop. Every once in a while he makes a gulping sound. He is simply retrieving some of the food reserve from his crop. On a much cooler night than tonight, he would have to shiver to produce enough energy to keep himself warm. The only bodily function that is not affected by torpor is the grasping reflex that enables a bird to stay on its perch while sleeping.

And so our little hummer is all settled in for a night of rest and renewal. In just a few weeks it will be time for him to start south on a long, long journey that will take him nonstop across the Gulf of Mexico, or overland to parts of Central America. For now, all he has to be concerned about is getting through the night.

After a few hours of darkness, dawn breaks on the trumpet vine and lantana. Our little hummer awakens, jump-starts his heart, and begins increasing his body temperature with his morning calisthenics. Soon all his bodily functions are restored to normal, and the day's rituals begin all over again.

"There is little question that migration is an evolutionary development that has favored the survival of the birds able to meet the demands of an ever changing world."

Gordon M. Snyder,
"The Wonders of Bird Navigation" in *The Gift of Birds*

"First-year hummingbirds, including the ruby-throated, migrate alone rather than with parents or experienced birds. They are born with an innate sense that tells them when to fly, what route to take, how heavily to feed, where to rest, and when to stop."

Connie Toops, *Hummingbirds: Jewels in Flight*

SIX

Long Day's Journey into Night: Migration

To me, the observation of birds is exciting in every season of the year, but undoubtedly, the most thrilling times of all are in fall and spring. Then occur mass movements of entire populations of certain species of birds from one location to another—in many cases, from one hemisphere to another. This occurrence, called migration, is filled with mystery, beauty, and wonder.

One of the most intriguing mysteries of migration is how birds find their way over thousands of miles of terrain that is bound to change dramatically from time to time. For example, forests are cleared, mountains are literally removed, new highways stretch across the land, new skyscrapers punctuate the horizon, ancient buildings are demolished and disappear from the landscape, and rivers are rechanneled.

How does that tiny atom of birdlife, the Ruby-throated Hummingbird, find its way year after year from hundreds of miles south of the border to the same branch of the same tree to rear its young or to the same nail where its favorite sugar-water feeder hung the previous year? Even more amazing is how the fledgling, no more than two or three months old, finds its way the first time it migrates south to its winter home. It has no guide. It has no parent or sibling to accompany it on the long, hazardous journey. It has no map to show it the route or where the best sources of food are located. Instead, it makes what seems to humans an impossible passage all alone. Nancy Newfield says, "Young birds migrating for the first time must rely on untested, inborn navigational skills to reach a winter home they have never seen."

The very word "migration" conjures up images of north- or southbound Sandhill Cranes by the thousands, calling to one another as their lazy-V formations crisscross the heavens; wildly honking geese heading for watery nesting grounds or grain-filled wintering grounds; the plaintive "kip-ip-ip" of Upland

Sandpipers whistling in the night; soft wispy notes of warblers floating through the treetops; flutelike songs of thrushes moving through the woodlands; and the repetitious, yet musical, "pill-will-willet" of Willets, lake-hopping their way between Tierra del Fuego and Alaska or Canada.

Almost lost in the overall picture of these mass movements are the tiny hummingbirds as they make their way on their own, one by one, between wintering and nesting grounds. Yet, theirs is one of the most impressive stories of all.

As a general rule, in the huge family Trochilidae, not many species of hummingbirds migrate at all. The vast majority spend their entire lives within rather limited areas, some of them never wandering farther than ten miles away from their natal sites. As with all rules, there are exceptions. Two notable exceptions among our North American hummers are the Rufous and Ruby-throated Hummingbirds. Of the fifteen species of hummingbirds that occur on a regular basis north of the Mexican border, the Rufous Hummingbird may be the champion of long-distance migration. After nesting as far north as southern Alaska, it makes a journey of at least 2,500 miles between Alaska and Central America twice each year. Not far behind the rufous in terms of distance is the Ruby-throated Hummingbird, traveling at least 2,000 miles twice each year between wintering and breeding sites.

The most sobering thing about the migration of the ruby-throat is that for many individuals, 500 to 600 miles of that journey is nonstop across the Gulf of Mexico. How in the world is it possible for so tiny a creature—barely a tenth of an ounce of feathers, skin, and bones—to muster the stamina to make such a journey? There are no fast-food stops along the way, no in-flight refueling, no rest areas, no one to commiserate with when the weather becomes lousy en route—just one small package of energy against the power of the rolling waves, gale-force winds, and torrential rain. How do they do it?

In short, the hummingbird body is a veritable power plant. It has the capacity to take on what Crawford Greenewalt calls its "migratory fuel supply." At this time in a hummingbird's life, it enters a phase called hyperphagia, a time of feeding frenzy when the bird spends much more time than usual ingesting nectar and small insects. During this time, hummingbirds have an astonishing ability to put on extra body fat, 50 percent to 100 percent of their normal weight, to be used as fuel during this period of strenuous migratory exertion. In human terms, Greenewalt continues, "it is as if a 170-pound man could in a few weeks put on enough fat to increase his weight to 255 pounds (or even 340 pounds) against some extraordinary and short period of exertion during which he could neither eat nor sleep."

Bob Sargent, hummingbird bander from Alabama, notes that hummers can double their weight in as little as seven to ten days. He says when he handles birds that have fattened up for migration, they feel "downright squishy" between his fingers, like soft butter.

Ornithologists who have studied hummingbird flight speed and energy expenditure calculate that 2.1 grams of fat accumulated through hyperphagia is sufficient to enable a hummingbird to fly close to 800 miles without having to stop to feed. This information explains why rubythroats are capable of the nonstop journey across the Gulf of Mexico.

In our mind's eye, let's follow one young-of-the-year female Ruby-throated Hummingbird as she makes her way on her initial jaunt from the place where she was born in Manitoba to central Costa Rica, where she will spend the northern winter months. I don't know for a fact that a hummer born this year in Manitoba would attempt to go all the way to Costa Rica, but just for the sake of the story, let's assume that it would.

Let us begin the saga at Winnipeg in Manitoba, near the geographic center of North America. Let's say our hummer was hatched in a nest in Assiniboine Park six kilometers west of downtown Winnipeg. The 160-hectare park is Winnipeg's largest and most popular outdoor facility with diverse habitats including lawns, gardens, and bur oak and river-bottom forests. With all this ideal habitat, together with the adjoining Assiniboine River, the park attracts a large number of species of birds, especially during migration. Its abundant flowering plants and waterway provide a perfect setting for a Ruby-throated Hummingbird's nest.

It is mid-June when our little hummer first sees the light of day in the English garden near the south bank of the river. On the fourth of July, her tiny toes grasp the side of the nest, which is almost identical to the one in Cameron Park in Waco, where I observed the entire nesting cycle. From there she stretches, flutters her wings, releases her tight grip, and takes her first flight of no more than a few feet, before clumsily landing on a nearby tree. For the next 30 days or so she perfects her flying skills, and her mother continues to assist her in getting food. During that time the mother teaches her to forage on her own as she explores blossoms in the surrounding area of the park to determine which ones offer the richest rewards in nectar. Additionally, the mother teaches her to drink from a sugar-water feeder at park headquarters. Finally, the mother senses that her offspring is ready to be on her own and drives her out of her feeding territory, since her progeny is now a major competitor for food.

Soon the young hummer finds a territory of her own nearby, still in the park, and defends it from all who would intrude, even her own mother. Under her mother's tutelage, she has learned survival skills that will stand her in good stead in the coming weeks and months and, indeed, for the rest of her life.

Southward Migration

On a day in mid-August, when she is scarcely two months old, something tells her that it is time to depart her natal environs. Day length is probably the factor that interacts with the hummingbird's system to trigger this irresistible urge to migrate, an urge that demands that she leave the security of the only home she has ever known and head due south. Little does she know of the perils she must face on the long and arduous journey that lies ahead. Upon awakening on this day, she feeds heavily for several hours, and for reasons she doesn't compre-hend, she heads south into the great unknown.

After five and a half to six hours of flying, she becomes hun-gry and weary and stops when she sees a field of wildflowers. She doesn't know it, but she is somewhere near the banks of the Sheyenne River in eastern North Dakota. Here she spends her first night away from home. The next morning she awakens early, feeds heavily all morning, and flies south again for several hours in the middle of the day. Since she is a creature of the daylight, she finds another suitable place to feed and rest for the night. This time her nighttime roost is in southeastern South Dakota, a few miles south of Sioux Falls.

With forward flight speeds recorded between 45 and 60 miles per hour, let us assume our prodigious traveler can fly at a sus-tained speed of approximately 45 miles per hour for a period of five to six hours on these forays as she heads ever southward. Doing so, each travel day's jaunt covers approximately 270 miles.

Flying low, she can see brightly colored flowers and red-trimmed sugar-water feeders as she makes her way through east-ern Nebraska, Kansas, and Oklahoma. Every once in a while she drops down to take a sip and rest a few minutes or a few days, according to the weather conditions, before going on.

Sometimes on this wearisome journey, the hummer has to stay in one place for several days because of inclement weather. At this time of year, frequent cold fronts move southward across the continent from Canada. During early fall in 1995, one such cold front delivered an unseasonable snowfall in Kansas, Okla-homa, and the Texas Panhandle during mid-September. Had our little hummer been caught in such a front, she might have spent three or four days in the area, going into torpor not only during the night but also during some of the colder hours of the day to preserve her energy. On the other hand, sometimes these cold fronts with accompanying north winds actually aid the hummer in her southward excursion, giving lift to her wings and speeding her on the way with a strong tailwind.

By the first of September the traveling hummer has made it to Central Texas and finds a welcome sight, the Turk's cap that flourishes at the corner of a house (thanks to the birds that planted it there in the middle of a holly bush). In addition, there are two sugar-water feeders in the yard that the resident diligently maintains throughout the migration season and well into the winter months. Here the hummer finds respite for a few days.

Where does she find refuge at night? Perhaps in the holly bush at the other end of the house. Since it is near the feeders, sometimes she perches there during the day. Sitting on one of her favorite perches, the wire basket above the feeder in front of a window, she guards her source of sustenance throughout the daylight hours. Sometimes as many as five different hummers, all immatures like herself, jockey for food at one feeder. Nevertheless, she remains the dominant bird and chases away the others the minute they attempt to feed. Once in a while, when she is caught up in one of these chases, another hummer sneaks in for a long sip of the energy-giving mixture. The other hummers, like herself, are simply trying to make it to their winter home.

Since the male Ruby-throated Hummingbirds leave their breeding grounds one to two weeks before the females and immatures, she doesn't have to compete with them for the necessary food supply during migration. The other females and the immature birds give her enough trouble. Once in a great while, a straggling adult male turns up, like the one I saw as late as September 21, 1995, at my home. The dominant female quickly dispatched him, and I never saw him again.

Finally, about the middle of the second week of September, our little hummer arrives at the Gulf Coast around Rockport and Fulton, Texas. Her journey has taken her on a vector due south from Winnipeg to Rockport, a distance of roughly 1,500 miles. Here she finds an abundance of trumpet creeper vine, lantana, Turk's cap, firecracker bush, and other flowers that are attractive to hummingbirds. If she were capable of a thought process, she probably would think she was in hummingbird heaven. In reality, she is in the Bird Demonstration Garden planted especially for hummingbirds and other migrating birds

Hummers feed heavily before heading south across the Gulf of Mexico during migration. Photograph by Curtis E. Williams.

that migrate through this part of Texas. She spends the next seven to ten days here, along with scores of other migrating rubythroats, adding the necessary fat to fuel the longest flight of her entire life, her nonstop flight across the Gulf of Mexico or the lengthy overland flight to the innermost reaches of Central America.

On a day that is marked by a stiff northerly breeze and sunny skies, she departs the continental United States alone, flying close to the tops of the waves. Occasionally she drops down into the swells for a few moments of respite from the wind. Undoubtedly, many hummingbirds perish at sea during migration in the hurricanes or tropical storms that plague the gulf at this time of year. Only one-half to three-quarters of young hummingbirds survive to reach adulthood. This hummer is one of the lucky ones that lives through the hazards of her first migration.

After a sustained flight of ten to twelve hours, the hummer is little more than halfway to landfall. Darkness overtakes her as she flies steadily onward through the night. Finally, as dawn breaks, she sees land. It is the northern coast of the Yucatan Peninsula. What a welcome sight it is. Her long day's journey into night has carried her into a warm, tropical, sunlit morning. She lands and feeds on the many flowers in bloom before finding a safe place to nap off and on for the rest of the day. In her exhausted condition she would be easy prey to any predator that came along, so her resting place must be well hidden.

The next morning she awakens to a dawn chorus of unfamiliar bird sounds. After stretching her tired, aching muscles, she takes flight and feeds ravenously again on the abundant supply of nectar-rich blossoms that seem to be all around her. After she spends several days in this tropical paradise recovering from her long energy-depleting journey, she continues on her southward quest for a winter home.

After flying, resting, feeding, and sleeping her way through the Yucatan, Guatemala, Honduras, and Nicaragua, she finally finds herself at a coffee plantation in central Costa Rica. Around the hacienda there are nectar-rich flowers galore, but since she is just a visitor in these environs and thus subordinate to the resident species, competition for food is more fierce than it was in the place from which she came. Here she is not able to hold one specific feeding territory. Rather, she must wander into the resident tropical hummers' space and poach her daily sustenance. Here she ekes out an existence that is a far cry from the park in which she was born in Winnipeg, where her kind was the only hummingbird species. However, subsist she does, until sometime in late March, when her inner alarm tells her it is time to move north, back to her natal home.

Once again she must fatten up to have enough fuel to power a journey that to humans seems impossible. To make the cycle complete, she must retrace her path to the coast of Yucatan and back across the formidable Gulf of Mexico, then on to Canada where she was born. And so ends the imaginary journey of one Ruby-throated Hummingbird. From the facts that we know of hummingbird migration, it could well happen exactly as told here.

From the East comes an unusual account of rubythroat migration that was related in "The Flower Kissers" by Robert Finch in the July 1990 issue of the magazine *Diversion*. In this report Finch says that Peter Sauer, executive director of Wave Hill, a cultural institution that examines the relationship between culture and nature, told him of this interesting event. Sauer says that every September the passage of Ruby-throated Hummingbirds through the concrete canyons of Manhattan is bizarre. On some days large numbers of rubythroats may be seen on West 252nd Street in the Bronx. After following patches of jewelweed down the banks of the Hudson River, they make their way through the Bronx down the Harlem River and through East Harlem by stopping and eating at blossoms in flower boxes that are set in the windows of apartment buildings. Then the birds fly through Central Park and continue down flower-bedecked Park Avenue. Here they are seen flying no higher than ten to twelve feet above the traffic.

When they reach the barrier formed by the Pan Am Building at Grand Central Terminal, Sauer says, "fragmentary evidence suggests that the hummingbirds hang a left over to Third Avenue. At this point, many of them seem to become exhausted and give out, landing on the pavement in the vicinity of 950 Third Avenue." It just so happens that this is the address of the headquarters of the National Audubon Society. It is reported that members of the staff go out and gather the exhausted hummers from the pavement and take them inside for rest and recuperation. The hapless waifs couldn't pick a better place to collapse.

From the Associated Press comes the story of another hapless waif, one that hitched a ride south on an airplane in 1996. A resident of Huntington, Vermont, found the tiny rubythroat with a broken wing and took it to Carol Winfield, founder of the Vermont Wildlife Rehabilitators Association. Under Winfield's care the hummer recovered from the broken wing, but not in time to fly south when other hummers were migrating. Instead, the lucky little rubythroat flew to Texas in a cage on the lap of Julie Young, a student at Texas A&M University, Winfield said. There it was reunited with other hummingbirds that were on their way south. I applaud Continental Airlines for waiving its standard $50 fee for pets that ride in the cabin with their owners.

Northward Migration

Just as in the fall, males depart their winter homes in Central America and Mexico before their female counterparts. They arrive in the southern United States a week or two before the females, then fly on to wherever they intend to establish their breeding territory for the coming season.

Ornithologist Paul Kerlinger noticed a difference in feeding habits of migrating male and female Ruby-throated Hummingbirds while he was conducting a study of transgulf migrant songbirds on a Mississippi barrier island. He noted that the males arrived two weeks ahead of the females, and invariably they established feeding territories around thistle plants blooming near freshwater marshes. He said they defended these against all other hummers as well as against nectar-sipping orioles that were migrating through at the same time.

Kerlinger reported that when the female rubythroats arrived, they went to scrub and pine woods habitats where their main source of nectar was greenbrier blossoms. Further, he stated, the females moved into the thistle habitat only after the males had migrated farther north.

In the spring, North American hummers follow their favorite flowers north as they bloom, the same as they follow them south in the fall. Even though cool fronts that come through during early spring may delay the blooming of certain flowers, the birds usually arrive on time anyway. My next-door neighbor in Waco, Lorene Atwood, keeps a calendar of hummingbird activity. She says the first rubythroats always arrive in our neighborhood around March 20, so we make a practice of putting out our sugar-water feeders no later than mid-March. Maryanne Newsom-Brighton, a nature writer who lives in Indiana, reports that the Ruby-throated Hummingbird arrives in southern Indiana the first week of May no matter what the weather conditions. She says that in some years the early-blooming quince and sugar-water feeders that people put out are crucial to the survival of birds that arrive before the flower season is in full bloom.

Why do hummers move north in spring? It is the promise of nectar-filled flowers and the availability of mates that draw them northward, but at the northern limit of their breeding range, the Ruby-throated Hummingbird often arrives a month or more before the nectar-bearing plants are in full bloom. How, then, do they survive? During the interval, rubythroats are known to take advantage of the holes drilled in sap-bearing trees by sapsuckers.

The Yellow-bellied Sapsucker arrives in the north at about the same time as Ruby-throated Hummingbirds. The sapsucker drills spiraling sets of holes around the trunks and larger limbs of living trees, waits long enough for the sap to rise, goes back to the trees, and imbibes the sap and eats the insects that accumulate there. The rubythroat, in like manner, goes to these holes and drinks the sap, which simulates the nectar of flowers in that it has about the same ratio of sucrose and amino acids as nectar. The hummers also eat the small insects that collect there. In a study conducted in Michigan by William Foster and James Tate in 1966, it was discovered that 20 different species of birds visited the sap holes. They also discovered that ruby-throats were the most frequent visitors, and they came to drink and eat even more often than the sapsuckers that drilled the holes. In some of the literature on hummingbirds, this bizarre habit is described as "the sapsucker connection." Indeed, northern distribution of the Ruby-throated Hummingbird during early spring may depend on the availability of sap from the Yellow-bellied Sapsucker's drilling.

In another study in northern Michigan, in 1972–1973, E. E. Southwick and A. K. Southwick discovered that during the nesting season, females fed almost exclusively on tree sap and rarely took nectar. All six nests that they studied were within 300 meters of a sapsucker feeding tree. Their laboratory studies indicated that the birds could be fully supported by the feeding trees, which contained phloem sap at a concentration of 16 grams of sugar per 100 grams of solution. All the trees in this study were paper birch *(Betula papyrifera)*. Southwick and Southwick concluded that in northern Michigan, Ruby-throated Hummingbirds are energetically coupled to the feeding trees of Yellow-bellied Sapsuckers and thus achieve reduced energy costs in this northern climate due to the proximity of this food resource to their nests.

Southwick and Southwick observed a brooding female continuously for two days and occasionally on other days during the nesting season. They noted that other than the visits to the feeding tree, she made few excursions away from the nest site. They timed her trips to the feeding tree and discovered that she almost always went directly to the tree in 1.8 to 5.8 seconds. Her return trips to the nest almost always followed a zigzag pattern, which took her approximately 18 seconds.

In the book *A Complete Guide to Bird Feeding*, John V. Dennis notes that sapsuckers, in turn, frequently drink from hummingbird feeders.

It is astounding to me how hummingbirds are able to adapt in order to survive. I fully agree with Gordon M. Snyder when he says, "There is little question that migration is an evolutionary development that has favored the survival of the birds able to meet the demands of an ever changing world."

Hazards

Aside from the dangers hummingbirds encounter on migration, a hummingbird faces untold hazards every day of its life—obstacles that we as humans cannot even begin to imagine. They run the gamut from domestic cats to hawks to inclement weather. It's a wonder any of them survive.

Their size and maneuverability in flight enable hummingbirds to escape the grasp of most predators, but sometimes a hungry hunter takes one by surprise. I have never witnessed this personally, but one observer saw an American Kestrel catch a Ruby-throated Hummingbird while it fed at a bed of zinnias. Scott Shalaway reported seeing a Sharp-shinned Hawk pick off a Ruby-throated Hummingbird in midair. There is at least one record of the remains of a rubythroat found in the stomach of a Merlin.

One of the most surprising of captures by another bird is reported by Alexander Skutch. He says a male Baltimore Oriole seized and killed a male Ruby-throated Hummingbird that was hovering in front of the same flower at which the oriole was trying to feed. Skutch also relates that in September 1948, two rubythroats were seized by praying mantises while visiting blossoms, one in Pennsylvania and one in Texas. In each case a woman was watching; the hummer in Texas survived, but the one in Pennsylvania perished in the insect's stubborn grip.

Jean Schwetman writes a weekly column, "Nature Notebook," in the *Waco Tribune-Herald* in Texas. She wrote this story, which was passed on to her by one of her readers. The reader first saw a praying mantis perched in a bush near a hummingbird feeder and had no idea that the insect was a threat to her hummers. One day, to her horror, the woman found a hummingbird clutched in the pincerlike front legs of the predatory insect. The woman wanted to warn others to remove mantises they find on branches near sugar-water feeders. The insect hunts by waiting, motionless, for the approach of prey. Then, when its quarry appears, the insect goes into lightning-fast action, grasping and holding fast its unsuspecting prey.

A spiderweb, one of the hummer's primary sources for nest materials, can be a death trap for the inexperienced or careless hummer. To gather spider silk the bird must fly to within inches of the vertical, wheel-shaped web. Suspended in space before the web, the hummer hovers while it attempts to pluck strands of silk from the web with its bill. Often it gets too close and its whirring wings become enmeshed in the sticky strands, rendering the bird helpless. As a result of this type of mishap, many a Ruby-throated Hummingbird has died of starvation or exhaustion before it was discovered by a human.

Arthur Cleveland Bent reports some accidents that involved Ruby-throated Hummingbirds and spiderwebs. Ralph E. Danforth told him about a rubythroat that was caught in "a pendulous mass of cobweb," from which he freed it with some difficulty. Another story involves a man's hearing the distressful cries of a rubythroat. When he investigated he found the bird hung in a spider's web that was attached to a rosebush. The owner of the web, "a big yellow-and-brown, pot-bellied, bloodthirsty rascal," was in the process of winding the web about the bird. The hummer's wings and legs were already tightly wound in the web. The man untangled the hummer and set it free.

In Corpus Christi, Texas, Pat Swartz once found a Ruby-throated Hummingbird caught in the web of a golden garden spider at her home. Pat took a broom and gently rolled the hummer out of the web. It flew off unhurt.

Another of Bent's stories came from Joseph Janiec, who was wandering through a large hollow one June afternoon when he noticed the unusual waving of a pasture thistle. He said there was no breeze at the time, so he went over to investigate. He found a male rubythroat, with its stomach feathers stuck to the prickly purple flower, struggling to free itself. The man removed the little bird and it promptly flew away unharmed, although it lost a few feathers in the process.

There is even a record, from California, of an unidentified hummer that was captured by a bass, of all things. The hummer was hovering over a lotus pool when all of a sudden the fish jumped out of the water and swallowed the bird whole. Large frogs in ponds and along stream banks also catch humming-birds that are hovering nearby.

Bill Hilton of York, South Carolina, declares that bullfrogs have big mouths. He says they normally take mice, crayfish, other frogs, and small snakes, but they are also known to snatch hummingbirds right out of the air if they come too close to the frogs' territory.

Besides the praying mantis threat, rubythroats also need to beware of dragonflies. Alexander Skutch relates a story of a huge dragonfly in Ontario that caught a rubythroat by the neck and held it on the ground until some people arrived and drove the insect away, thus saving the hummer's life.

Picture windows sometimes pose one of the greatest hazards to hummingbirds. Flowering plants and sugar-water feeders that are placed too near a picture window invite crashes, especially when quarreling hummingbirds become too rambunctious. Hummers see the reflection of plants and trees in the glass and think they can fly straight through to the other side; too often they break their necks when they collide with the glass. One source that I read suggested placing a fine-mesh window screen over such windows. However, on one occasion that I remember at our house, I discovered a rubythroat with its bill stuck in the window screen. Luckily, I found it and set it free before it died.

Insecticides used by gardeners sometimes act as double jeop-ardy to hummingbirds. Small insects and spiders comprise a significant portion of a hummingbird's diet. Indiscriminate use of pesticides may not only kill the insects hummers seek, but it may also cause the death of the birds themselves when they feed from flowers that have been sprayed.

Another warning to gardeners: be extra careful during nesting season that you do not prune off a nest-bearing branch. This is easily done, since a hummer nest is so tiny and sometimes looks like a knot on a small limb. Maryanne Newsom-Brighton suggests that you might just want to hang up those pruning shears until fledglings appear at the flower beds.

Sometimes humans go to extraordinary lengths to protect hummers. A few years ago, when an electric-fence manufacturer produced red insulators to attach wires to metal posts, hummingbirds were drawn to the red, inserted their beaks into the hole containing the metal rod, and were electrocuted. Random inspection of fences equipped with these red insulators revealed one hummingbird death for every five insulators. John Wylie, then a staff member with the Missouri Department of Conservation, said that whole family units, adults and young, were killed.

As soon as word of this reached birders, they rose up in arms and made phone calls and wrote letters of protest, asking the manufacturer to change the insulator color. To help speed up the remedy, hundreds of hummer lovers went into action and, with the permission of property owners, tromped along miles of electric fences, spray-painting the red markers in colors that would not attract hummingbirds. Unfortunately, these insulators are marketed all over North America and in Central and South America, covering the geographical distribution of all hummingbirds.

Honey is another human-induced hazard to hummers. Thinking honey is a more healthful substitute for sugar, many people have offered it as an alternative to sugar water, only to find it is lethal to the hummingbirds. Expert opinion now indicates that a straight diet of honey water can cause fatal fungus conditions on the birds' tongues. Honey also contains botulism toxin, another toxin that hummingbirds do not encounter in natural nectar. According to John V. Dennis and Pat Murphy, "When bees manufacture honey, they convert the natural sucrose in flower nectar to an invertase sugar, primarily dextrose and fructose. Hummingbirds prefer sucrose sugar." Also, honey water spoils more quickly than sugar water. So, please, no matter how healthy you consider honey in your own diet, do not use it as a substitute for sugar in the food supplements you offer hummer visitors at your home.

"Hummingbirds are one of nature's most intricate extravagances."

Robert Finch, "The Flower Kissers"

SEVEN

The "Hummer/Bird Celebration!"

Several monuments have been erected to honor North American birds. The first one was a plaque commemorating the extinct Passenger Pigeon in Wyalusing State Park, Wisconsin. Another is the Gull Monument on Temple Square in Salt Lake City, Utah, in honor of the California Gull for its part in easing the effects of the great Mormon cricket plague of 1848. The Mormons credited the gulls and divine providence with saving their people from almost certain starvation. The world's first monument to a songbird, the Kirtland's Warbler, was unveiled on July 27, 1963, in Mio, Michigan, in the heart of the limited nesting range of this endangered species.

So far as I know, there is no monument anywhere in the United States or Canada in honor of the Ruby-throated Hummingbird. There is, however, an annual educational event that is dedicated to the uncanny migratory feat of the rubythroat's nonstop passage across the Gulf of Mexico twice each year in spring and fall. The event is called the "Hummer/Bird Celebration!" and it is held each September in the coastal townships of Rockport and Fulton, Texas. Two separate towns that run together, Rockport and Fulton have a combined population of 7,300 and are located 35 miles north of Corpus Christi and 60 miles south of Victoria in the Coastal Bend.

The first "Hummer/Bird Celebration!" was in September 1989. The organizers didn't know what to expect in numbers of attendees, and they were surprised and quite pleased when 200 folks showed up for the festivities in a building with no air-conditioning. The next year they moved the celebration to a larger building that was air-conditioned, and 800 people attended. The third year they had to add another building when 1,500 people registered. Finally, in 1992, they moved the celebration to the Aransas County Independent School District's junior and senior high school complex to accommodate the growing crowds. There they found a permanent home.

The towns of Rockport and Fulton on the Texas coast host the annual "Hummer/Bird Celebration!" Photograph by June Osborne.

Huge concentrations of hummers cluster around feeders during migration. Photograph by Curtis E. Williams.

The number of attendees keeps climbing. It was reported by the chamber of commerce in Rockport-Fulton that a record 5,000 people participated in the celebration in 1996. The visitors spend millions of dollars for the weekend each year, a welcome addition to the region's economy during its off-season. How did all this start? Rockport birders Dan and Betty Baker were birding with Jesse Grantham in Bayside one day during fall migration in 1988 when they noticed huge concentrations of hummers clustered around hummingbird feeders in the residential area. At the time Grantham was headquartered in Corpus Christi as manager of the National Audubon Society's Texas Sanctuary System. Since then he has moved to California and now serves as assistant director of Audubon sanctuaries for the West.

Grantham says that when he and the Bakers saw the spectacular concentrations of hummers, he began to wonder how they could share such an event with others. From the beginning, Grantham thought the charismatic Ruby-throated Hummingbird could be the vehicle for encouraging people to have a greater appreciation of nature and for creating in them a desire to protect and preserve wildlife in their own back yards.

On that day in 1988 the idea for the "Hummer/Bird Celebration!" was conceived. Soon the Bakers and Grantham took the idea to the chamber of commerce that serves both towns on Aransas Bay. Betty Baker says it didn't require much selling of the idea, since the two cities had already learned the economic value of avian tourism from the wintering Whooping Cranes at the nearby Aransas National Wildlife Refuge. The people at the chamber readily agreed to help promote the celebration.

That first year they had four speakers and a few guided field trips to see the birds. In anticipation of the tenth annual event in 1998, they were expecting more than 5,000 participants to hear speakers from all over the United States, all experts in their fields, who *came* to educate, delight, stimulate, and entertain.

The "Hummer/Bird Celebration!" is not a money-raising project of the chamber of commerce. It is a nonprofit event staged by more than 200 volunteers, including the chamber staff and their families. It is designed to pay for itself and to make no profit. If any profit is generated, it is returned to the community to support nature-related projects.

The celebration is not run like a convention as such. Rather, it is a coming together of people with like interests for the purpose of learning about and viewing not only migrating hummingbirds but all birds in general. No preregistration is required, but it is a good idea to make motel reservations well in advance. There is something for everyone. The programs, workshops, and nature tours are designed for all levels of interest, from novice to expert—for anyone with an intellectual curiosity to learn more about the natural world that surrounds us. The celebration has welcomed all ages since 1994, when they added programs for the younger set.

The cost of attending this celebration is nominal. At the time of this writing, participants could pay $2 at the door for each program they attended, and they could buy individual tickets from $5 to $20 for workshops or boat or bus tours. There are few other entertainment events in the world that offer such a bargain.

The original purpose of the celebration was to mark the passage of the huge numbers of Ruby-throated Hummingbirds as they stop in Rockport-Fulton at feeders and nectar-producing plants on their southward journey to Mexico and Central America, where they spend the winter. It has turned into much more than a celebration. It is an outstanding example of ecotourism at its best. Ecotourism is designed to bring in monies to the economy of a town, while at the same time educating people, especially local people, on the need to protect and preserve whatever natural resource is the focal point. In this case it is the Ruby-throated Hummingbird and its habitat.

Betty Baker says that when the organizers displayed posters to advertise the first celebration in 1989, local business people thought they were crazy. After they saw the response that first year, they became believers and started asking what they could do to help promote the idea. The promoters of the celebration began presenting programs in the area throughout the year to educate local people on how they could help preserve the natural resources that were already there and enhance the situation by planting additional native plants. Local residents soon started planting flowers and shrubs in their yards to attract the hummers, and they hung more and more hummingbird feeders. Shortly after that, the Texas highway department got into the act. With the help of local volunteers, the agency planted a demonstration hummingbird garden at an existing picnic area on Highway 35 North that goes through Rockport and Fulton. The Texas Parks and Wildlife Department, Texas Water Commission, Aransas County Clean Team, University of Texas Marine Science Institute, Rockport Islanders, Rockport Home and Garden Club, Texas Maritime Museum, and a long list of other groups and individuals joined forces to bring the garden into being.

The demonstration garden is divided into three parts. The far garden is devoted to plantings that attract butterflies and hummingbirds, such as firecracker bush, Cape honeysuckle, hummingbird bush, Mexican Turk's cap, Mexican bush sage, Texas scarlet bush, lantana, autumn sage, Mexican butterfly weed, and many more. The middle garden is given over to native plants that also attract a variety of migratory and resident birds. The third part is a freshwater pond, stocked with freshwater fish to attract migrating waterfowl.

It is hoped that people who view this garden will want to incorporate the many varieties of plants, shrubs, and vines into their own back yards and thus increase available habitat for all migratory birds, at the same time beautifying their landscapes. The idea has caught on. People all over the two towns and the surrounding area have planted hummingbird flowers in their yards, and through the educational programs they now know the importance of protecting existing habitat and maintaining clean hummingbird feeders.

The demonstration garden is managed and maintained by the Friends of Connie Hagar, Inc., an organization dedicated to preserving the history of a tiny wren of a lady who put Rockport and Fulton on the birding map of the world. Additionally, the Friends further public awareness, interest, knowledge, understanding, and appreciation of the life and habitats of the birds of the Texas Coastal Bend (specifically the Rockport-Fulton area) as exemplified in the life of Connie Hagar, through research, education, and acquisition of properties.

Connie Hagar was born Martha Conger Neblett on June 14, 1886, into an aristocratic family in Corsicana, Texas. Connie, as she is affectionately known, moved to Rockport in 1935 with her husband, Jack Hagar, after spending a month in Rockport with her sister in 1934. During that visit she became aware of the diversity of birdlife in the area. As a result, her main reason for wanting to live there was to "study the birds." In order for Jack to have something to do while she pursued her passion for birds, he ran what came to be known as the Rockport Cottages—a motel-style complex of nine small, white, one-room dwellings, which he remodeled.

Beginning in 1935, for more than 35 years, Connie made twice-daily rounds of the same nine miles, recording her observations of birds. At first, ornithologists from the Northeast did not believe her reports of rare bird findings. Finally, she persuaded them to come and see for themselves. When they did, they couldn't believe their eyes. It didn't take long to convince them that she knew what she was talking about. Through the years the guest register at Rockport Cottages became a veritable who's who of North American ornithologists and birders, who came to see for themselves.

This incredible woman's life is profiled in Karen Harden McCracken's book *Connie Hagar: The Life History of a Texas Birdwatcher.*

From 1935 until about 1970, Connie Hagar recorded 500 species of birds in the Coastal Bend area of Texas. Ever since then, thanks to the untiring efforts of this dedicated woman, Rockport and Fulton have been known as a birder's paradise and a naturalist's Mecca.

Connie Hagar died November 24, 1973, leaving a legacy to the birding world that is unparalleled. She is buried under a live oak tree in a cemetery in Rockport, beside her beloved husband, Jack, who preceded her in death. The simple headstone marking her resting place hardly seems adequate to commemorate her monumental contributions to ornithology, but the sanctuaries in Rockport and Fulton that carry her name are an ongoing legacy.

The Connie Hagar Cottage Sanctuary was dedicated during the seventh annual "Hummer/Bird Celebration!" on September 8, 1995. Roger Tory Peterson, world-renowned bird artist, author, and guru of birding as we know it today in North America, was invited to be the keynote speaker for the ceremony. His presence was particularly appropriate, since Peterson was one of the many nationally and internationally known birders and ornithologists who visited the Hagars on the site. During his speech at the dedication, he reminisced about those visits in the thirties. Between those visits and Peterson's death in 1996, he wrote or edited some 50 field guides, which have been translated into fourteen different languages.

As early as the fall of 1938, Connie Hagar noticed huge concentrations of hummingbirds gathering at flowering plants at the upper end of Live Oak Peninsula, which divides Copano and Aransas bays. She noted that from there they moved southeast to Mustang and Padre Islands, offshore from Corpus Christi. In a single day she counted up to 3,000 rubythroats. Such mass movements of rubythroats are unparalleled elsewhere.

Although they far outnumber the others, rubythroats are not the only hummers that are seen here. In addition to the rubythroat, four other hummingbird species have been recorded as they pass through the Coastal Bend area on migration: Rufous, Broad-tailed, Black-chinned, and Buff-bellied. The first three are considered western and mountain hummingbirds, and the Buff-bellied is a visitor from Mexico and the Rio Grande Valley.

This phenomenal movement of hummingbirds that Connie Hagar discovered remained a well-guarded secret outside Rockport until some 50 years later, when Jesse Grantham and the Bakers came along. They thought it was too good to keep under wraps any longer, and so the "Hummer/Bird Celebration!" was born.

The format of the annual event is simple: educational programs, boat and bus field trips, booths with bird paraphernalia, and keynote speakers. Of course, the hummers are the main attraction, but other birds are celebrated as well. Rockport and Fulton are known worldwide among birders as one of the birding hotspots in North America. It is in Aransas National Wildlife Refuge that endangered Whooping Cranes spend the winter. The refuge is just a few miles from Rockport and Fulton.

Nancy Newfield, master bird bander from Louisiana, began a five-year hummingbird banding project in Rockport during the "Hummer/Bird Celebration!" of 1992. She set up her banding operation in specified locations each year, and every day during the celebration, people observed her and her assistants as they trapped and banded these little flying jewels. The project studied the age and sex ratios of the hummers and evaluated their physical condition during migration.

According to Newfield, "The massive migration of Ruby-throated Hummingbirds through the Rockport-Fulton area has been well-documented but little studied. Banding these birds can provide a broad spectrum of interesting and important data."

After recording all the data and banding each hummer, Newfield would allow an observer to hold the tiny bird before it was released. I was one of the lucky ones in 1997, when she allowed me to release an immature male rubythroat. It is awesome to see such beauty and iridescence at close range. Additionally, it feels as if you are holding in your hand a miniature mechanism with its motor racing. When you open your hand, it usually takes a second or two for the bird to realize it is free to go. When it does, its wings start rotating at an enormous rate, and before you know it, the little dynamo of nature is airborne and out of sight.

There are now more than twenty birding festivals located all over the United States at different times of the year, celebrating such birds as eagles, pelicans, avocets, cranes, ducks, shorebirds, warblers, and others. Other communities that have special birds would do well to take lessons from these endeavors.

Why is the "Hummer/Bird Celebration!" so successful? The

Master bird bander Nancy Newfield sets up her banding operation in specified locations each year. Photograph by June Osborne.

organizers, headed by Betty Baker through 1995 and Cynthia Womack since 1996, are still scratching their heads over that question. They think the main reason is that people are hungry for the high quality of programming they have so far been able to maintain. Of course, the hummers are the main attraction, but they found out in 1991 that even when the birds don't show up for their party, the celebration can still be successful. A week before the festival that year, a cold front came through, and the birds left by the thousands. By the weekend of the celebration, there were hardly any hummers left in the coastal area, but the people came and enjoyed the programs and field trips anyway.

Whatever the reasons for success, people keep coming back year after year. They come from all over Texas, from many other states, and even from as far away as Canada and Japan. All agree, the "Hummer/Bird Celebration!" is a unique experience in honor of a unique little bird, the Ruby-throated Hummingbird, truly "one of nature's most intricate extravagances."

"Every bird I hold in my hand is special, each like a mystery novel."

Susan R. Blackshaw, bird bander

EIGHT

Hummingbird Banding Projects

*I*n America we call it banding. In Great Britain and Europe they call it ringing. No matter what name you give it, the practice of placing aluminum bands on the legs of wild birds in order to learn more about their movements and behavior has the potential of teaching us many things about individual birds, species, and families of birds. Some of the things we've already learned through this method are times of migration (seasonal movements), routes taken and destinations (including distances traveled), population trends, length of life, and weights of individual birds at the beginning of migration.

Some other areas of study for hummingbird banders include breeding-site fidelity, strays or extralimitals (birds away from their normal migration routes), nectar source preferences, and recovery data. Some hummingbird banders pursue extensive scientific research in more specific areas of study. For instance, Ellie Womack, an Oklahoma hummingbird bander, has an intense interest in extralimitals and albinos. Many questions about the migration of hummingbirds remain unanswered. Today master bird banders are working diligently to unlock some of the mysteries that persist.

In the United States the banding of migratory birds is administered by the Fish and Wildlife Service; in Canada it's done by the Canadian Wildlife Service. Not just anyone can obtain a permit. Applicants for a master-personal banding permit in the United States must be at least 18 years of age. They must provide the names of three active banders or recognized ornithologists who are able and willing to vouch for the applicant's ornithological, mist-netting, and record-keeping ability. Some applicants work as apprentices for a time with someone who already holds a permit. The applicant must provide a well-developed study plan showing a valid need for a banding permit.

Nancy Newfield, master hummingbird bander in Louisiana, says the third requirement is extremely important. She explains

This partial albino made a brief appearance in Wimberley, Texas.
Photograph by Luke Wade.

that the study plan should specify a need for specific information that cannot be obtained without a hands-on approach. The
proposed study should justify the collection of such information based on its benefit to the species or to the people of the
United States. Researchers who wish to band hummingbirds
require a special dispensation added to their permits to qualify
them to band hummers. Applications are available from:

> Chief, Bird Banding Laboratory
> Office of Migratory Bird Management
> National Biological Service
> 12100 Beech Forest Road
> Laurel, MD 20708-9619

If you find any dead or injured bird (not just a hummingbird) that has a band on its leg, you should call 1-800-327-
BAND (2263). The caller should give as many details as possible,
such as date, location, condition of the bird, weather—anything
that might be helpful. If the caller can identify the bird, species
information is beneficial but not crucial. The Bird Banding Lab
can find out the species through the bird's band number.

As recently as twenty years ago, fewer than a dozen bird banders were qualified and licensed to band hummingbirds. Our
knowledge of hummingbird behavior has increased dramatically as the number of licensed, active hummingbird banders
has increased. According to Ellie Womack, editor of *Hummingbird Hotline* (a newsletter for hummingbird banders), at the
time of this writing there are 42 active master permit holders,
including 1 in Canada, 1 in Jamaica, and 2 in Puerto Rico.
Additionally, many subpermittees are making major contributions in the field of information-gathering; however, their reports still must go to the Bird Banding Lab under the master
permit.

As one would expect, a majority of master hummingbird
banders operate in the western states, such as Arizona, where
one may see as many as fifteen different species of hummers.
The Nature Conservancy's Ramsey Canyon Preserve in southeastern Arizona is one of the prime locations for banding hummers. Here hummingbirds are captured one morning and

evening each week from late spring through fall. Only those guests with reservations on the sanctuary grounds may observe this work.

Biologist Sheri Williamson, master bander, formerly banded hummingbirds at the Ramsey Canyon Preserve. While there she used a four-posted net the size of a small room. The birds were enticed into the room by a sugar-water feeder suspended at the entrance. After they got a drink, they flew into the loose net. Williamson had an assistant who retrieved the birds for her so they did not have to remain trapped long enough to become traumatized.

While Williamson weighed and measured the tiny birds, a volunteer record-keeper jotted down the vital statistics. After Williamson placed the miniature aluminum band on the bird's leg, the tiny captive was given a reward of another drink of sugar water before it was released. The entire process took about five minutes, and the same procedure is used by other hummingbird banders.

Williamson says that the infinitesimal hummingbird bands tell a whopping story. If banders catch a bird that has already been banded, they can look up its numbers to see when and where it was previously examined and how much it has grown.

The bands that are used are so tiny, I don't know how in the world the bander picks them up, much less attaches them to the tiny birds' legs. Ellie Womack sent me a notecard with some hummingbird bands taped to it. When flat they are approximately one-quarter of an inch long and one-sixteenth of an inch wide. Each tiny band has a letter and five numbers embossed on it, such as T12345, to identify the individual bird.

Ellie Womack obtained her master permit in December 1985 after serving one and a half years as a subpermittee. The bands that were being used at the time were designed by Don Bleitz, now deceased. They were called X-bands (*X* for experimental) and were made of black-anodized aluminum. They were the first bands approved for hummers, and they were actually smaller than the next issue by millimeters. Womack says the next issue of bands was of a different type, with the outlines a bit larger than the original design.

The Bird Banding Lab soon issued a recall in response to the concerns of some banders who felt the new, somewhat larger bands might cause injury to hummingbirds. Womack's supervisor, Jim Johnson, had already noticed the difference in size and had instructed Womack to trim the bands very close to the numbers and to cut the length just shy of the mark. It was when the Bird Banding Lab issued the band recall that she decided to volunteer her services to help remedy the situation.

Womack had already persuaded George Jonkel, then chief of the Bird Banding Lab, to send her the names of all hummingbird banders. From that list of 53 names, she found only 13 who were actually banding hummingbirds. After the band recall, Womack persuaded the Bird Banding Lab that it was more a bander problem than a band problem. She asked for permission to become Communications Central by offering her phone to deal with future problems and volunteering to publish a newsletter. Thus was born *Hummingbird Hotline*. Issue Number 1 appeared in September 1986.

Womack took it on herself to write instructions for forming hummingbird bands, and she sent them to all banders and to the Bird Banding Lab, which then agreed to rescind the band recall. Following Womack's suggestions, the lab now prints bands in series of 100, with 10 across and 300 to a sheet, as opposed to 420 to a sheet with 14 across. Her goal is to have the rows slitted to improve the quality of cutting. For a long time hummingbird banders had to guess at how to cut and shape the bands. Not even an instruction sheet or drilled pliers were available at first. Womack's written instructions and the smaller bands were a major breakthrough.

Then Womack contacted Roger MacDonald, who was making banding pliers for other types of birds, to see if he had hummer banding pliers. MacDonald told her he was willing to try to come up with some if she would send him some bands. She sent him unnumbered aluminum strips, and coincidentally, about the same time, Jack Murray, who lived a short distance from MacDonald, also contacted MacDonald. At the time, Murray was working with some researchers in Arizona on hummer banding. Womack supplied measurements and tested MacDonald's original cutter, which was now much improved, while Murray made hands-on suggestions. When MacDonald came up with the present cutter, shaper, and pliers, it was another major advancement. Ellie Womack is hesitant to take any credit for the improvements. She says these things would have happened eventually with other participants, but she just happened to be the one who volunteered her efforts to keep things moving. Indeed, I am sure hummer banders in all parts of North America are grateful to all those who had a part in these improvements. The gigantic advances help banders do a better job with our Lilliputian dynamos of nature.

In the East, a dozen dedicated master hummingbird banders are actively involved in banding the Ruby-throated Hummingbird, since it is the main hummer that inhabits the eastern two-thirds of the United States and Canada.

Bill Hilton, hummingbird bander, says that he doesn't know for sure if the rubythroats that spend the summer in his yard in York, South Carolina, migrate to Mexico or Central America in early fall. He does know that none of them overwinter around York and that they begin moving out in late August. All of them are gone by October 18.

Hilton gets reports of rubythroats in large concentrations gathering in Florida and at other locations along the Gulf Coast beginning in early September. A few weeks later, he starts hearing reports from observers as far south as northern Panama, who are seeing large numbers of Ruby-throated Hummingbirds arriving in their area. Since the species is present in the tropics only during the northern winter months, Hilton concludes that this is convincing evidence that the Ruby-throated Hummingbird does, indeed, migrate as far as Central America.

One of the most fascinating aspects of hummingbird banding to me is the recovery data. Not only do they reflect the distances and routes traveled by individual birds but they also tell us a lot about the ages of hummingbirds. Ellie Womack says that we have learned through banding that Ruby-throated Hummingbirds live much longer than we previously thought. She has records of two rubythroats that reached at least age eight years. Womack says "at least" because these birds were adults (at least one year of age and possibly older) when banded. Womack also has records of two rubythroats that reached at least age nine. One of the two was banded as an immature in 1980, making its known age nine when last captured in 1989. The other rubythroat actually may have been older than nine, as it was mature when banded and there was no way to determine its exact age.

In a paper published in the *Oklahoma Ornithological Society Bulletin* of December 1994, Womack reports some notable recaptures of Ruby-throated Hummingbirds. She states that from 1976 to 1990, Fred and Marguerite Baumgartner operated the Little Lewis Whirlwind Nature School and Sanctuary near Jay, Oklahoma, where Marguerite banded almost 3,000 Ruby-throated Hummingbirds. During the summer of 1991, after the Baumgartners moved to Georgia but before the property was sold, Womack banded an additional 131 Ruby-throated Hummingbirds at the sanctuary. Besides those Womack banded, she retrapped 13 hummingbirds that had been banded by Baumgartner. One was an adult female banded June 19, 1986, and recaptured by Womack July 26, 1991, making it at least six years of age. On July 12, 1991, Womack banded an adult male Ruby-throated Hummingbird at the sanctuary. On July 23, 1994, she recaptured the same bird at her home in Grove, Oklahoma, approximately 20 miles away. Womack says of the recapture, "While not an unexpected distance for a hummingbird to roam or a particularly unusual age for a male hummingbird to attain, actually encountering a banded individual of this age at a site this far removed from its original banding location three years later is, indeed, a rare and exciting event."

According to the bird banders that I have talked to, banding birds can be fun, but it is also hard work. Most bird banders are volunteers with the National Biological Service in Maryland, the federal agency that tracks indigenous animal populations. Tax dollars pay only for the bands, reporting forms, and data manipulation at the receiving end. All means of capturing the birds—nets or traps—are acquired at the expense of the individual bander.

Many hummingbird banders use nylon mesh nets that resemble very fine badminton nets. Called mist nets, they are used to capture a wide variety of birds ranging in size from hummingbirds to jays. The Japanese originally used them to capture birds for eating. Consequently, they came to be known as suicide nets, because any bird captured in them in Japan was destined to end up in the cooking pot.

Other hummingbird banders use traps that resemble birdcages. They may hang a sugar-water feeder in a location that will attract hummingbirds—perhaps near blooming flowers. When the birds are accustomed to coming to the feeder, the bander will then place the sugar-water container inside one of the traps in the same location. The opening has a trip wire that the bander manually operates from a few yards away as soon as a hummer enters the cage. Banders then walk over to the contraption and gently remove the bird with their hands. Neither method—mist nets nor traps—harms the birds in any way.

I am told that banding birds has a magical quality. Banders always live with the anticipation of capturing a bird that was banded by someone else in an area that may be miles from where it is recaptured. They always hope that a new bird, one that is not supposed to be in their area, will show up in their nets or traps. Susan R. Blackshaw says that banding birds is much like putting a note into a bottle and throwing it into the ocean. There's no telling where it will eventually come to rest.

Because of their Lilliputian size, perhaps it is not so surprising that few banded hummingbirds are ever recovered. Hummingbirds are so small, it is easy for human observers to overlook them. I remember only two occasions in my 23 plus years of birding when I have found dead hummingbirds. Both were rubythroats without bands. One was in my own back yard. The other was at a friend's house. Most birds that meet an untimely death or even death by natural causes are probably consumed by natural scavengers almost immediately after their demise, leaving no chance for humans to find them.

Ellie Womack relates the story of an adult male Ruby-throated Hummingbird that she banded on August 28, 1992, in Grove, Oklahoma. The bird was found dead in Carlton, Minnesota, on

June 22, 1993, a distance of about 625 miles due north of the banding site. Although this obviously doesn't tell the whole story for the bird, its recovery revealed one of the longest known distances traveled by a banded Ruby-throated Hummingbird. Womack speculates that more than likely she captured and banded the bird on its way south in 1992, and it died after it wintered somewhere in Central America and returned to its nesting area in Minnesota the following year. Although only a small percentage of hummingbirds banded are recovered away from their original banding site, a high percentage (from 10 percent to 25 percent) are recaptured at their banding site in subsequent years.

As bird bander Susan Blackshaw says, each bird is "like a mystery novel." How long will it take to solve all the mysteries of the lives of these dynamos of nature? Most likely we shall never know all the answers.

"Let a man plant a flower garden almost anywhere from Canada to Argentina and Chile, in the lowlands or mountains, amid humid forests or in irrigated deserts, and before long his bright blossoms will be visited by a tiny, glittering creature that hovers before them with wings vibrated into twin halos while it sucks their sweet nectar."

Alexander F. Skutch, *The Life of the Hummingbird*

NINE

Hummingbirds in Your Garden

*F*eeding birds has become big business in recent years. A 1991 U.S. Fish and Wildlife survey found that 63 million Americans spend more than $2 billion on this activity each year. The survey also discovered that more and more people are feeding birds year round.

In the summer, hummingbird feeding is a fascinating and popular pastime for bird-watchers, nature lovers, nature photographers, and for all who take delight in sheer beauty. Perhaps one reason it has become so popular is that it is so easy to lure hummingbirds to our yards and gardens. There is also the somewhat-justified feeling that we are helping hummers by feeding them.

Hummingbirds have such a high metabolic rate and expend so much energy in their daily activities that they must eat every ten minutes or so to survive. Naturalist Edwin Way Teale said it succinctly when he observed that the hummer must be—of necessity—"a bird in a hurry." If humans had the same metabolic rate as hummers, they would have to eat more than 100 pounds of food per day. Thank goodness, that is not necessary; but since hummers require so much food, what can we do to keep them humming?

The best way I know to help the hummingbirds of your area is to attract them to your garden or yard. Basically there are two ways of accomplishing this: go the artificial route and put out hummingbird feeders, or take the natural way and plant flowers, shrubs, vines, and trees that are attractive to hummingbirds. Since my husband and I are not gardeners, we chose the artificial route a long time ago.

Artificial Attraction

When I first became interested in birds in 1975, I lamented to one of my friends, a more experienced birder than I, that I had no flowers in my yard. I told her I wanted to see hummingbirds up close and personal, but I was afraid I would not be able to do so since we had no flowers to attract them. She told me, "No problem. There are more ways to lure hummingbirds than digging in the dirt and weeding flower beds. All you have to do is buy or make a hummingbird feeder, boil a sugar-water solution, pour it into the feeder, hang it near a window so you can see it, and voilà, you should have hummingbirds."

I tried it and it worked. Here are some steps you need to take to be successful at this project.

THE RIGHT FEEDER

There are as many different kinds of hummingbird feeders as there are manufacturers who make them, but when you get right down to it, the hummers really don't care whether the feeder is ceramic, plastic, glass, or pottery or whether it is elaborately or simply decorated—just so long as the juice is fresh, accessible, and reliable. Hummers are known to travel as far as one mile to visit a reliable feeder. Bob and Martha Sargent, licensed bird banders who specialize in hummingbird research in Alabama, think hummers can see the red on your feeder from about three-fourths of a mile. The key is to find the feeder that suits your needs and the hummingbirds' needs best. Here are some rules to keep in mind when choosing a feeder.

First and foremost, a feeder should be attractive to hummingbirds, and the main thing that makes one attractive is simply the color red. For a long time people thought it was necessary to add red food coloring to the sugar water to attract the attention of hummingbirds. Then some years ago there was a scare about red food dye causing harm to hummers, and at the time hummingbird experts advised us not to add the coloring. Since most commercial feeders come with red on them somewhere, whether it is red flowers, a red cover, a red spout, or a red base, there is really no need to put red food coloring in the sugar-water in the first place.

Second, the design of the feeder should be simple so it is easy to take apart and clean. When looking at different feeders in the store, ask the attendant for permission to take the feeder apart. Make sure there are no inaccessible crannies that are impossible to reach with a cleaning tool such as a percolator brush or a pipe cleaner. A feeder that cannot be thoroughly cleaned may harbor fungi and bacteria that will sour or ferment the solution and thus be harmful to the hummingbirds.

Third, the feeder should be functional even on windy days, when the liquid it holds may slosh about and spill on the ground. You want a feeder that does not leak so the solution is not wasted. Those feeders that have a downspout are particularly prone to lose the liquid on windy days; that is the main reason I personally do not like to use that type of feeder.

In looking through the many bird-feeding supply catalogs that I receive, I see that there is an array of names for the feeders almost as interesting as the birds' names. There are feeders called HummZinger, HummBerry, Hummingbird Circus, Window Tube for Two, Four-Flower Frolic, Four Fountains, Nectar Bar, Etched-Glass Hummingbird Chalice, and Hummer Station, to mention a few. Basically, there are two types: tube and bowl. The tube type comes in several varieties and sizes, with or without flowers, perches, bee guards, and downspouts. The bowl type comes in different shapes and sizes and with different numbers of nectar ports, anywhere from four to eight, with or without bee guards.

The tube-type feeders with flowers, perches, and bee guards are easy to take apart and clean. The perches give the birds a chance to rest while they feed and give you a longer time to watch these little flying jewels. Furthermore, it would take a gale-force wind to shake the liquid from this type of feeder. The bee guards are not perfect, but they help keep the bees away for a time.

Hummingbird feeders are widely available in feed and seed stores, pet shops, hardware stores, lawn and garden centers, discount stores, supermarkets, some department stores, and specialty gift shops. Also they may be ordered from many mail-order catalogs.

As a last resort, you may choose to make your own feeders from test tubes, pill vials, small glass containers such as baby food jars, or hamster water dispensers. I've even seen them made from ketchup bottles. Almost any small glass or plastic container will do. If you go the do-it-yourself route, just remember to put red on the receptacle, either by painting a band of red across the top with nail polish or tying red ribbon around the container.

THE SUGAR-WATER RECIPE

The sugar-water solution that most nearly simulates flower nectar is one part sugar to four parts water. In other words, if you use one cup of sugar, add four cups of water. Bring the mixture to a boil for two to three minutes to kill bacteria and mold spores. Boiling also causes any chlorine or fluorine in the water to evaporate, and the solution will stay fresh longer. Allow it to cool before you fill your feeders. Store any leftovers in a closed container in the refrigerator.

Some writers suggest that you begin with a stronger solution—one part sugar to two parts water—and after the birds get used to coming to your feeder, dilute the solution according to the recipe above. There is some danger that this stronger mixture may cause enlargement of the birds' livers and possible dehydration in the birds that drink it. To avoid any risk of harm to the birds, I always use one part sugar to four parts water.

There are commercial mixtures of instant nectar on the market today. Even though there is nothing in them that actually harms hummers, many hummingbird authorities do not recommend them. They say they contain ingredients the birds don't need, and too, they are relatively expensive. Nancy Newfield, a well-known hummingbird authority who lives in Louisiana, says that none of the commercial mixtures provide better nourishment than a simple homemade sugar syrup. The birds get all the vitamins, minerals, and proteins they need from the natural nectar, the sugar water at your feeders, and the insects they eat, so why bother to go to the extra expense?

Under no circumstances should you substitute honey for sugar. Contrary to popular belief, honey is composed of an entirely different type of sugar from that found in the sucrose nectar that hummingbirds normally consume in nature. Honey has been proven to be harmful to hummingbirds. Honey used in a hummingbird formula spoils quickly and has a tendency to become contaminated with a fungus that is harmful to the tiny birds and can eventually kill them. So please *do not use honey* in your hummingbird feeders. Fructose sugar and corn syrup are unsatisfactory. Brown sugar is not greatly different from refined sucrose, but artificial sweeteners are deadly to hummers. Under no circumstances should you use them.

If you choose to go the sugar-water feeder route, be forewarned. In any given hummingbird season, you could use an awful lot of sugar. John Hillman of Cape Fair, Missouri, feeds the birds more than 250 pounds of sugar in one season. Using the ratio of one part sugar to four parts water, that would make 125 gallons of nectar. John estimates that it takes about 1,000 visits by hummers to consume 1 gallon of nectar a day, and he says some days they've gone through as much as 2 gallons. Each of his feeders holds 36 ounces of liquid. In his words, "In a year's time I feed sugar to untold thousands of voracious hummingbirds." Apparently, his home is on a heavily traveled migration route.

Bob and Martha Sargent of Alabama maintain 51 sugar-water feeders in their yard. They say their hummers consume 2.5 gallons per day. Bob laughingly says that when they go to the grocery store to buy sugar, the clerks must think they are in the whiskey-making business.

FEEDER MAINTENANCE

Once you begin feeding hummingbirds, it is important to keep the solution pure and the feeder clean. During hot weather it is best to change the solution every two to three days, because during long hot summer days the solution can sour in a short time. At the first sign of cloudiness or milkiness in the sugar water, you should pour it out, wash the feeder in hot soapy water, rinse it well, and refill with a fresh preparation.

The best tools I have found to clean hummingbird feeders are a percolator brush, pipe cleaners, an old toothbrush, and a

BACKYARD FRIENDS

They greet me like gypsies
with an open-handed grace,
these hummingbird friends,
as they dart from leaf to feeder
with life and death urgency,

supping on healing ooze
from vibrant petals,
and on my home-made
people nectar.

Tracking the flying colors
of their frantic pace
causes me to do the opposite:
I slow myself, rally,
then unwind.

©Phyllis Williams, 1996

Feeders can be placed close to the house: "What *we* can see is what *they* get." Photograph by Barbara Garland.

bottle brush with soft bristles. The percolator brush and pipe cleaners fit into tiny holes and crevices that the bottle brush cannot reach. The toothbrush is good for cleaning mold off bee guards. The soft bristles of the bottle brush will wipe away any particles of mold or fungus that may have formed inside the feeder but will not scratch the inner surface of the feeder. There are now bottle brushes on the market that are especially designed to clean certain types of feeders.

Occasionally, if the bottle brush just will not scrape off stubborn bits of mildew or mold on the inside of the feeder, I pour a tablespoonful of dry rice into the opening, put a little water in it, and shake vigorously. The rice acts as an abrasive and scours the walls of the feeder. If you use this method, don't forget to rinse the feeder thoroughly after emptying the rice and water mixture.

PLACEMENT OF FEEDERS

A few years ago I taught a birding class in one of the senior centers in my hometown, Waco, Texas. One of the men in the class told me he placed feeders where he and his wife could see them while comfortably seated inside. He said, "What *we* can see is what *they* get."

This is a good rule of thumb to follow when deciding where to put your hummingbird feeder. I hang mine from the eave of the house a few inches from my office window so that when I glance over the top of my computer, the feeder is directly in my line of vision. The feeder should be placed in a location that is not in full sun all day. When it's in the shade for at least part of the day, the solution will stay fresh longer. There should be an open area around the feeder so the birds can dart in and out quickly without danger of colliding with something.

It is best to hang hummingbird feeders where they are at least partially protected from wind. On a windy day, not only does the solution slosh around and spill from certain types of feeders, but the swaying of the feeder also makes it necessary for the birds to expend a lot of extra energy just to get a drink from it.

It's not a good idea to suspend hummingbird feeders from tree limbs, because that makes it too easy for squirrels to get to them. Squirrels, too, guzzle sugar water at every opportunity and have been known to destroy feeders to get at that last drop of sweet stuff. If your feeder is attached to or suspended from a post, by all means use a squirrel baffle similar to those used for seed feeders. Any number of household items may be used for baffles: inverted aluminum pie tins, plastic gallon milk jugs with the top removed, garbage can lids, sheet metal fashioned into a cone, four-inch diameter PVC sewer pipe, old 78-speed records, and more. The idea is to make a barrier that the squirrel cannot get past, or one that the squirrel slides off of if it is ingenious enough to get past. To tell you the truth, it's almost impossible to outfox a squirrel, but I have found that the aluminum pie tin works well at my house. Split it from one side to the center, wrap it around the post, and tape it into place with duct tape or electrical tape.

Hummingbirds have a tendency to become territorial at a feeder and will guard it to the extent that other hummingbirds cannot get anywhere near it. If you want lots of hummingbirds you should hang more than one feeder. The best idea is to hang feeders in different areas of your yard so that a hummingbird can see only one of them at a time.

Last but not least, place the feeder high enough from the ground (at least 6 feet high) so it is inaccessible to cats. House cats do not pose a major problem for hummingbirds (as they do for songbirds), since the little dynamos are so fast they can usually flee from the grasp of a cat on the prowl. If a cat should become a problem for your hummingbirds, it's a good idea to place a small bell on the cat's collar. The noise from the bell will at least give the hummers fair warning when the cat is nearby.

OTHER SPECIES THAT ENJOY SUGAR WATER

There may be a bonus if you decide to go the artificial route. Did you know that worldwide there are more than 1,600 species of birds that eat nectar? It is possible to see more than 60 species of birds, other than hummingbirds, drinking sugar water at hummingbird feeders in the United States and Canada. In different parts of the United States I personally have seen Hooded, Scott's, Altamira, Audubon's, Spot-breasted, Streak-backed, Black-vented, and Bullock's orioles, as well as House Finch, Tufted Titmouse, Carolina Chickadee, Summer Tanager, Painted Redstart, Orange-crowned Warbler, Verdin, and House Sparrow. Other birds reported at hummingbird feeders include swifts, woodpeckers, jays, nuthatches, wrens, mockingbirds, thrashers, robins, grackles, cardinals, grosbeaks, and buntings.

Recently I watched a pair of House Finches as they explored the possibilities of getting a drink from a new hummingbird feeder I had hung in my front yard. It was a tubular glass feeder with red plastic flower spouts and no perches. At the beginning there were bee guards on all four ports, and the female finch couldn't seem to figure out the best way to get a drink as she perched atop one of the flowers. Her bill was too thick to probe the tiny openings in the bee guard to reach the nectar. When I saw her plight I decided to try to help her and removed the bee guards from two of the ports.

Later that day I saw the male House Finch drinking from one of the guardless ports while the female was eating sunflower seeds only inches away. She seemed to be watching his every move and soon displaced him at the hummingbird feeder to try her luck. Unfortunately, she went to the two ports where the bee guards were in place, and she was still unable to obtain a drink. It was not until the next day that she finally figured out the solution to her problem. She and her mate are now regular visitors at the two ports without bee guards, and I hung another feeder for the hummers.

Creatures other than birds also enjoy drinking at hummingbird feeders. Moths and butterflies frequently imbibe there. In Waco, I have watched a green anole, a type of lizard, as it lingered on the lip of a flower port. I couldn't decide which it was enjoying most—drinking the nectar or eating the small insects that were attracted to the sticky liquid.

In southeastern Arizona I saw a coati (*Nasua narica*) climb over the roof of a house and hang from the eaves while he reeled in a feeder that was suspended there by wire. He drained the bottle, seemingly with much delight. Raccoons and squirrels are notorious for emptying feeders, squirrels by day and raccoons by night. Also several species of bats drink sugar water. Raccoons and squirrels sometimes wreak total destruction on plastic feeders in their efforts to get at the sweet liquid. The moral of this story is, if you wish to reserve the sugar water exclusively for the birds, take in your feeders at night to prevent the night creatures from stealing the nectar and perhaps even destroying them. On the other hand, if you want to keep the night visitors happy, too, take in your hummingbird feeders at night and replace them with open-topped containers filled for the other critters. You can make these from baby-food jars or pimiento jars—any small jar that has a wide mouth. Fill them with sugar water and hang them at an angle with a perch nearby. You may even wish to have a spotlight trained on them so you can enjoy the after-dark show.

PROBLEMS AT THE FEEDERS

Sooner or later almost everyone who hangs a hummingbird feeder will experience one kind of problem or another. It may be ants, bees, wasps, yellow jackets, or some of the animals already mentioned if you perceive one of them as a problem. Most of these problems can be solved with a little ingenuity and a few helpful hints from those who have experienced the same difficulty at their feeders.

The consensus on the best way to get rid of ants that crawl down the wire supporting a feeder points to a moat of sorts on the wire above the feeder. You can actually buy contraptions that are made for this purpose. They are called ant traps or ant guards in bird supply catalogs and are simply small plastic cups with a hook at the center top and one at the center bottom. The idea is to fill this cup with water and place it above your feeder to deter the ants that crawl down the wire to get to the sugar water. Ants are incapable of crossing a water barrier without becoming trapped, so this method proves to be quite effective.

You could easily make such a contraption with a tuna or

Vienna sausage can, or any can of similar size. Just punch a hole in the bottom of the can, thread the wire through the hole, and plug the hole with epoxy glue. Suspend the feeder from the bottom of the receptacle. Fill the can with water, and you have an ant trap that is almost foolproof. Just remember to refill it every few days.

Another popular solution to the ant problem is to smear the wire with Vaseline, petroleum jelly, or vegetable or mineral oil to make a slippery or gooey surface on which the ants cannot gain a foothold. To be effective, application of these substances should be repeated every week or two. Bob and Martha Sargent suggest that you dip a pipe cleaner in vegetable oil and wrap it around the wire from which the feeder hangs to discourage ants. They warn that you should change it every week or so to keep it fresh. Donald and Lillian Stokes say Tanglefoot may solve the problem. This is a sticky substance that is sold in garden stores; the ants' feet get stuck in it when they try to crawl down the wire. Just remember to change it every week or so to keep it oily.

Bees, wasps, yellow jackets, hornets, and other flying insects cause a more difficult problem than the ants do, simply because their approach to the feeder is on the wing, the same as the hummingbirds for whom the feeder is intended. First, let me tell you what not to do. Never use insecticides on or near hummingbird feeders, no matter how critical you think your problem is. They can spell disaster for the hummingbirds. Try a more benign approach instead. Bee guards are effective in some instances, but if you notice they are no longer deterring the flying pests at your feeder, simply move the feeder to another location—perhaps within view of flowers that are natural attractants for those particular insects.

Another method that has been tried is a little petroleum jelly applied around the feeding port, but be careful not to get any of the substance inside the port. Someone suggested Vicks salve as a deterrent reasoning that the odor should repel bees because they have a keen sense of smell, but that it probably would not bother hummingbirds because their sense of smell is not so highly developed.

John K. Terres tells of a woman in Chapel Hill, North Carolina, who was troubled by bees and wasps at her feeders. She moved the feeders out of the sun, where the insects seemed to be most active, to a shaded area and turned on her garden sprinkler so it would hit the feeders. She said this deterred the insects and at the same time washed the sticky solution from the outside of the feeders. An added attraction was getting to watch the hummingbirds as they flew back and forth, bathing in the fine spray.

A friend of mine in Waco said that one year, all of a sudden, she began to see lots of honeybees at her feeders. Sometimes they were so thick around the feeding ports that they formed large balls so heavy that they actually fell to the ground. Finally she discovered that her neighbor across the street had brought one of his beehives home from its usual location in the country, and it was his bees that were emptying her feeders several times a day. As soon as her neighbor took the beehive back to the country, things returned to normal at her feeders.

HISTORICAL HUMMINGBIRD EXPERIMENTS

The first records we have of anyone's trying artificial methods of feeding hummers are from the latter part of the nineteenth century. In 1889, Caroline G. Soule of Brookline, Massachusetts, noticed that when the nectar supply became low in the flowers in her garden, the rubythroats could no longer reach it by thrusting their heads into the flower tubes as they normally did. Soon the enterprising little birds developed the habit of slashing open the petals at the base of the tubular flowers and drinking the nectar from there.

Soule tried to think of a way to help the birds. One day she got the idea of making an artificial flower to simulate the flowers in her garden. She wrapped her paper flower around a small vial filled with a mixture of sugar and water. She wired this in a natural position among a cluster of trumpet creeper flowers, then stood back to see what would happen. Soon a hummingbird discovered this artificial source of nectar, and Soule said it looked as if the little bird could not believe its good fortune. It returned time and time again to the paper flower and seemed to favor the elixir it found there over the real thing so much so that she had to refill the vial at least twice a day to keep the bird supplied.

Then Soule decided to try another experiment. She went to the garden, took the sugar-filled vial off the trumpet creeper, and stood nearby with it in her hand. Sure enough, when the bird showed up, it went directly to the vial in her hand and sipped, seemingly unafraid of Soule's close presence.

Sometime around 1890, a young girl who was convalescing from an illness in California entertained herself in the garden by holding out tubular flowers filled with a sweet solution she made. Soon two male hummingbirds were eating out of her hand. Those two early experiments probably marked the beginning of the artificial feeding of hummingbirds, and little about this art has changed or been improved on since then.

Hummingbird Gardens

Now, all you gardeners out there who wish to go the natural route, this section is for you. Numerous books have been written on the subject of landscaping your yard for the birds. There are far too many for me to list them here. Go to your local library or book store and you will see what I mean. In brief, I'll try to offer you a few practical suggestions on how to attract Ruby-throated Hummingbirds to your yard or garden with special plants, but for more details consult one of those books.

In sifting through some of the literature in my own library, variety seems to be the key in creating habitat that will attract hummers—variety in the plants you choose as well as variety in the places you decide to locate certain plants.

As with all other species of birds, four things are required to attract hummingbirds to your yard: food, shelter, water, and a perch with a view—one perch for the birds to rest on and to guard the feeder from, and one inside the house from which you may view the birds.

FOOD AND SHELTER

Some of the plants you choose to grow as food for hummers will double as shelter—a place to escape from predators, a place to nest and raise their young, or a place to roost for the night. Shade trees and large shrubs that are sheltered from the wind provide ideal nesting sites for hummers, especially when there is a reliable source of food nearby. When you are planning the layout of your plantings, remember to leave some open spaces where the males will have plenty of room for their magnificent courtship displays. Additionally, you may want to offer nesting materials for the hummers to use. They especially seem to like strands of human hair and the lint from clothes dryers. Such materials can be placed in an empty suet basket made of hardware cloth and hung in a tree or on a bird feeder post.

Natural food for Ruby-throated Hummingbirds consists of nectar from flowers and protein from insects. Insects from which hummers obtain protein include small beetles, weevils, bugs, flies, gnats, mosquitoes, aphids, leafhoppers, flying ants, and parasitic wasps, and they also eat arthropods such as spiders and harvestmen (daddy longlegs). Most of these may be found on or around the flowers and other plants that hummers visit for nectar.

Flowers that attract hummingbirds are likely to be scentless, since fragrance attracts competitors such as bees and butterflies, and hummers have a poorly developed sense of smell. A study at the Arizona-Sonora Desert Museum in 1989 discovered that 75 percent of the flowers that attracted hummers there were red. In some cases the flowers produced both red and orange or red and yellow blossoms. Typically, hummingbird flowers are red in color and tubular in shape, although there are exceptions to this general rule. Some flowers that are not red are high in nectar content. Conversely, some red flowers, such as roses, produce little nectar.

When you are ready to purchase plants to attract hummingbirds to your garden, the first thing to do is to choose from among plants that are well adapted for the region of the country in which you live. Plants that thrive in the Northeast, for instance, may not survive in the heat and humidity of the Gulf Coast areas. *Birdscaping Your Garden,* by George Adams, is an excellent book to consult. Adams tells the reader which plants grow best in which parts of the country.

Adams suggests that some of the best flowering plants for the Ruby-throated Hummingbird are columbines (*Aquilegia* spp.), trumpet vine *(Campsis radicans),* scarlet lobelia *(Lobelia cardinalis),* and any of the bee balms (*Monarda* spp.).

Nancy Newfield and Barbara Nielsen coauthored *Hummingbird Gardens.* They say that a carefully planned combination of flowering plants, shrubs, and trees will prove to be very attractive to hummers. Their book provides how-to information on feeders, plant combinations, and garden design for different parts of the continent.

Columbines are perennial plants that grow well on woodland slopes, rocky outcroppings, and in moist woods throughout the United States, except along the Gulf Coast. Wild columbine *(Aquilegia canadensis)* grows from one to three feet tall and has flowers that vary from light pink and yellow to blood red and yellow. It blooms between April and July. Crimson columbine *(Aquilegia formosa)* grows from two to four feet tall and has red and yellow flowers that bloom between May and August. It will grow in almost full sunshine or in shady areas.

Trumpet vine is sturdy and vigorous. It bears beautiful red or orange trumpet-shaped flowers between July and September. Trumpet vine thrives in moist woods, thickets, and roadsides from New Jersey south to Florida and westward to Iowa, Missouri, and Texas. It prefers a position in your garden with full sun.

Cardinal flower, commonly known as scarlet lobelia, is a beautiful perennial that rubythroats seem to love. It is usually two to three feet tall with tubular flower clusters borne on erect flower spikes. It blooms between July and October. It requires a well-drained, moist location in light to partial shade.

Bee balms are members of the mint family, and many of them have aromatic, minty leaves. There are twelve annual and perennial species that are native to North America. Those species that are red-flowered, for example, are particularly attractive to the Ruby-throated Hummingbird. It is a perennial and grows two to four feet tall and blooms from July to September. Bee balm may be found in moist meadows and thickets throughout the eastern United States as far south as Georgia. It thrives in slightly acidic soil in full sun or partial shade.

Honeysuckle is also known to be attractive to hummingbirds. One that you might consider cultivating in your garden is trumpet honeysuckle *(Lonicera sempervirens)*, commonly known as coral honeysuckle. A vine that is semievergreen to evergreen (in the South), it may reach 13 to 20 feet long. Its showy, trumpet-shaped flowers grow 1 to 2.5 inches long and are red with yellow centers. They bloom between April and September.

I have noticed in our yard that hummers are attracted to the blossoms of the mimosa trees *(Albizia julibrissin)*. Martha Sargent calls the mimosa "one-stop shopping" for hummers. Its blossoms provide lots of nectar, and they also attract a number of insects, a source of protein for hummers. Other trees suggested for their nectar-producing blossoms are crybaby tree *(Erythrina crista-galli)*, Japanese plum, loquat *(Eriobotrya japonica)*, or any of the citrus species.

Other plants that are good for rubythroats are firecracker bush, Cape honeysuckle, hummingbird bush *(Anisacanthus wrightii)*, Mexican butterfly weed, Mexican bush sage, firebush or Texas scarlet bush, lantana varieties, autumn sage, desert willow, jacobinia, scarlet sage, Mexican cigar plant, Indigo Spires salvia, Mexican honeysuckle, Turk's cap, Hall's honeysuckle, and shrimp plant. The list goes on and on. The ideal thing is to consult your nursery specialist or one of the books I mentioned and plan your plantings so you will have flowers in bloom throughout the breeding and migrating seasons of rubythroats.

For nesting sites, rubythroats seem to prefer any tree with lichen-covered bark over the relatively smooth-barked varieties. For example, in the upper piedmont and lower montane zones of South Carolina, they often choose lichen-covered post oaks *(Quercus minor)*. In the lower piedmont, where the oaks

A female drinks from a stream.
Photograph by Curtis E. Williams.

are more scrubby, pines and other tree species are more commonly used. Bob and Martha Sargent say most of the nests they have observed in Alabama were in pine trees. Farther north, in Allegany Park of New York, hornbeams commonly serve as nest sites, and in various other areas such species as hickories, gums, tulip poplars, junipers, yellow birch, sugar maple, red maple, beech, hemlocks, and others have been used.

WATER

Hummingbirds need water for the same reasons other creatures need water: for hydration and for bathing. An experiment using captive hummingbirds showed that they need four to five times as much water as solid food per day. Some individual hummers may consume up to eight times their weight in water daily. Most of it, of course, is obtained in the nectar they drink from flowers or from sugar-water feeders. In addition, they get some of their daily supply of water from dewdrops and raindrops on leaves, or from streams.

I don't ever remember seeing a hummingbird drinking water from a birdbath or bathing in a birdbath. This doesn't mean that they won't—I just haven't caught them in the act, but I have seen them bathing in the fine mist of a garden sprinkler. They make quick passes through the water, turn around, and come back to repeat the action. They do this several times until they are thoroughly doused, then they fly to a nearby tree and preen. They probably drink from the spray as well.

In natural settings they bathe and drink in the spray of waterfalls or on leaves of plants. Hummers, like other birds, seem to be drawn to moving or splashing water. They will choose pools or birdbaths with dripping water over still pools every time. If you want to see hummers at your birdbath, try putting a mister in the center of it. Either rig one yourself or look for them in bird supply catalogs.

I read somewhere that hummingbirds never bathe in rivers or streams. Well, I learned a long time ago never to say never when it comes to bird behavior, and I am here to dispel the theory that hummingirds don't use rivers and streams for the purpose of bathing. On two memorable occasions I saw hummers bathing in streams.

The first time was on a spring day in the Texas Hill Country several years ago. My friend Barbara Garland and I were driving over a low-water crossing on the Sabinal River when the movement of a very small bird at the edge of the water attracted our attention. Barbara stopped the car, and we focused our binoculars on a male Ruby-throated Hummingbird taking a bath. We sat spellbound and watched him for several minutes. From time to time he flew up into the spray caused by the rapid flow of water over rocks, then hovered above the spray and shook himself all over in midair. At other times he perched on a flat white rock in the middle of the river and dipped his head and breast into the water. When he found an isolated shallow pool, he submerged himself in the water and splashed droplets over his head and back. It was obvious to us that this was a pleasurable activity for this atom of birdlife, and it certainly provided the two of us a great deal of pleasure. It was a scene Barbara and I shall long remember.

On another occasion I observed hummers bathing in a stream in Costa Rica. My husband and I were with a tour group staying at a place called Rancho Naturalista. One afternoon we were treated to a performance that rivaled the water follies in the Esther Williams movies of long ago, only in this production the performers danced above the water for the most part, instead of in it.

We were led to a secluded spot at the top of a heavily wooded ravine, where there were benches for us to sit and watch the show. There was a shallow, spring-fed creek at the bottom of the ravine. The water was so clear, we could see every rock in the creek bed. Sun filtered through the thick foliage and danced on the sparkling water. The spring gushed out of a canyon a few yards upstream and formed five small pools just below our gallery of seats. Our guide gave each pool a number so he could announce which one to look in when a new performer entered the arena. A hush fell over our group, and not long after we were seated, the show began.

One after another the stars of the show appeared as if choreographed. A Green Hermit, 6 inches of glistening feathers and long decurved bill, normally lives in dense forest understory, but for us it came out of hiding and dipped in the clear water. We were captivated by its brilliant iridescent green feathers that were transformed to blue when it flitted through patches of sunlight.

A Crowned Woodnymph, at little more than half the size of the hermit, charmed us not only with its name but also with its deep violet crown, upper back, shoulders, and belly. Its chest was glittering green as if adorned with an emerald. It approached the surface of the stream gingerly, as if afraid of getting wet. It took a quick dip and flitted out of sight.

My two favorites were the Snowcap and Purple-crowned Fairy. The Snowcap has a shining white crown and a little white in the tail. Otherwise, it is deep wine-purple all over. At 2.5 inches, it is a sprite of a bird and could easily be missed in the deep shadows, but that snow-white crown grabbed our attention each time it flashed in the sun's rays. The diminutive bird hovered above the water and splashed down long enough to drench its breast and wings before fluttering away. It repeated this behavior several times while we were watching.

The Purple-crowned Fairy is an exquisite hummingbird of 4.5 inches. Tinker Bell, of Peter Pan fame, could have been patterned after this bird, with its exceptionally light and graceful flight. Watching this tiny fairy with the violet crown and velvety black mask was like watching a water ballerina. With elegance of movement, it pirouetted from one location to another as softly as a butterfly.

There were other hummingbirds and other kinds of birds that came to bathe in the stream that afternoon, but suffice it to say, don't believe it if you see it written or hear it said that hummers never bathe in rivers or streams. Take my advice: don't pass a woodland stream without at least checking to see what creatures might be bathing or drinking there. You may be privileged to catch performances of a lifetime.

Should you decide to construct a pool or pond for your hummers, just make sure the edges are shallow enough for the diminutive birds to stand in without being submerged. No matter how you choose to provide water for these sprites of the bird world—whether in natural streams or concrete ponds on your property, in sugar-water feeders, or in elaborate birdbaths with waterfalls, misters, or dripping water—I guarantee you'll be glad you went to the extra effort once you begin to see their aerobatic displays and water ballets.

A Perch with a View

Hummingbirds become very territorial around their favorite flowers or feeders. They find an exposed thin bare branch or a wire where they sit for minutes or hours to view their kingdom. Their heads sometimes look as if they are watching a fast tennis match when they move from side to side constantly. They are simply checking to see if anyone is invading their territory. They may become downright belligerent if other hummers attempt to drink at their feeder or flowers, and a chase ensues that rivals the dogfights of World War II. Often I get calls from people who are upset because they observe this behavior and conclude that hummingbirds are mean. I explain to them that the birds are simply doing what comes naturally—defending their source of food from interlopers.

Hummers usually have no trouble finding natural perches for this purpose, but I try to provide them with a convenient perch somewhere near the feeders so I can see them. Most hummingbird feeders come with a built-in wire for hanging. I wrap this wire around a hook and make sure there is enough left over to extend for an inch or two at a right angle from the hanging wire. This wire is just the right size for the hummingbird's tiny feet to grip.

It was just such a perch as this on which I observed a male Ruby-throated Hummingbird taking a sunbath one bright September afternoon only inches from my office window. Yes, hummers, too, enjoy soaking up some rays once in a while. When I first saw him, I thought something was wrong with him. I've seen numerous other birds in the process of sunbathing, but I had never seen a hummingbird practicing this bizarre behavior. He was sitting on the wire facing the window, and he bent his body almost in half (sideways) so that his head was leaning in the direction of my neighbor's house. His breast feathers were fluffed out on the opposite side in the direction of the sun, and his beak was wide open. He stayed in that position for a minute or so before he flew off, then he returned and assumed the same posture once more for another minute.

It is not known with certainty why birds sunbathe. One theory is that the sun helps get rid of parasites that find harbor in their plumage. Perhaps it just feels good to their skin when they are molting. Whatever the reason, I was glad I looked up from my own perch with a view at just the right moment to see this performance.

Let me remind you that one does not have to live in a large house with a huge yard to attract hummingbirds. If you live in an apartment and have a balcony or patio, or even just a window, your chances are just as good as those of the homeowner. My youngest son and his wife once lived in a small second-story apartment with a tiny balcony. They had a veritable garden in those few square feet of space on the balcony, with herbs of several varieties, tomatoes, flowering plants, and a ficus tree. They had three hanging baskets with red flowers, and after the flowers started blooming, they could hardly wait to see if hummingbirds would visit them. Sure enough, that first year, when migration time for hummers was upon us, the hummers came. For several weeks Sam and Laura saw male and female rubythroats as they passed through the Central Texas area.

With all the requisites in place—sugar-water feeders, flowering plants for food and shelter, water for hydration and bathing, and a perch from which to defend territory—you are now ready to sit back and enjoy the show from your perch with a view.

I shall not presume to tell you how to lay out the plan of your garden. There are plenty of books written on the subject, and it is not my intention to reinvent the wheel with this work. I simply want to let you know that you have the option of going two ways in order to attract hummers. Come to think of it, the most successful plan may be to combine plantings of flowers that are attractive to hummingbirds with careful and timely placement of artificial feeders.

No matter which method you choose, whether artificial, natural, or a combination of the two, when you see your first hummers buzzing around the feeders you have filled with sugar water or at the blossoms cultivated in your garden, you will be glad you went to the effort, because these enchanting birds will be around for a long time to entertain you with their dazzling colors and aerobatics.

Just as my family did, you may get to see their offspring when the mothers bring them to your feeder to teach them to drink from an artificial source or from the blossoms in your garden. You may recognize the early hummer that returns in the spring and curiously looks in the exact spot where the feeder was hung the previous year. This behavior may indicate that the birds remember from one year to the next the location of a reliable source of food. So why shouldn't we remember them?

Soon you will be able to recognize specific individuals by one characteristic or another. There may be a feather out of place, a patch of white where there should be none, a deformed bill, or some other outstanding feature. You may find that the same birds return year after year and you recognize them because of their distinctive features.

Through the years my family has named some of the hummers that habitually came to our feeders. One was Charlie Dancer, a male rubythroat with a habit of dancing all around the feeder before finally going to the port to drink. He reminded us of a Baylor wide receiver who adroitly danced around the field to evade the defensive team. His name was Charlie Dancer.

Then there was Ruffle Britches. She had a little row of white feathers that stood out just above the tops of her legs. We readily recognized her each time she came for a drink. Snowcap was a rubythroat with a patch of albino feathers atop his head. Had his body been dark purple all over, we'd have sworn the Snowcap (*Microchera albocoronata*) at the hummingbird pools followed us home from Costa Rica the previous spring.

One summer a young female rubythroat appeared at our feeder with a bill that was broken off at the halfway point. Her tongue extended far beyond the tip of her bill. When I first saw her I was afraid she wouldn't last the summer, but she stayed around for a surprisingly long time. Somehow she learned to cope with what we viewed as a hopeless handicap.

Another year a female rubythroat stayed all winter in our yard. We called her Vagabond Hummer. I had forgotten to take the hummingbird feeder down and noticed her on a cold day in November. Since there were no flowering plants around at the time, I cleaned the feeder and put new sugar water in it. On some very cold mornings I had to bring the feeder inside to thaw it out, but that little hummer remained with us until the migrating hummers returned in the spring. At that time she disappeared into the crowd and we could no longer recognize her.

Because of that incident I started leaving my hummingbird feeders out all winter. True, so far no other hummer has appeared at our feeders during the winter, but one never knows when a straggler might appear. If you decide to follow the same course, remember to change the solution from time to time so it is always fresh, and take the feeder inside on nights when the temperature is expected to fall below freezing. There's no telling what might show up there.

Winter Feeding

Once we thought hummingbird feeders must be taken down in late September to encourage the birds to go on with their migration. Mistakenly, we thought if we left them out the birds would stay just because there was a ready supply of food. Hummingbird authorities now tell us that the birds will leave when they are biologically ready to leave, no matter how many sources of food are available. Bob Sargent says that if a Ruby-throated Hummingbird is healthy, you would have to put it in a cage to keep it from migrating when it is time.

Now we know it's okay if we choose to leave feeders out until late in the winter, or all winter, for that matter, for tardy birds or a wanderer from another part of the country that might appear. Once a Rufous Hummingbird visited my feeder for one day in late October. Had I not left the feeder out long after the blackchins and rubythroats had departed, I would not have seen the rufous. Often, for reasons unknown, a hummer such as our vagabond winter guest is unable to make the marathon journey required during migration, and if no one has left out an artificial source of nectar, the bird will starve. Winter is also the time when unusual species of hummingbirds show up in places where they are not supposed to be.

If you choose not to leave your feeder out for the entire winter, wait for at least two weeks after you see the last hummer before you take it down. Who knows, you just might increase the survival chances of some late-hatching bird or an underweight hummer that didn't find sufficient nectar elsewhere to stock up for the journey across the gulf.

Hummingbird Decoys

If all else fails in your attempts to interest hummingbirds in your garden, you might try attracting hummers to your feeders with decoys, much the same as ducks and geese can be enticed to ponds or lakes. In one of the birding magazines I subscribe to, I found an advertisement for a hummingbird decoy. The manufacturer claims that if you place the decoy in a position with its beak in a feeder port or suspend it from a string or wire near your feeder, other hummers will get the message.

Perhaps our guiding philosophy should be: "If we put it out, they will come."

AIR SHOW

Just when I'm certain they're asleep,
the hummers begin again—
plunge from bud to branch
while I, with caught breath,
attend the sudden sink from sky to earth,
the dash from flower to feeder,
faster than hand, in utter amaze,
can fly to mouth.

© Phyllis Williams, 1996

Afterword

As I am writing at my computer,
a flash of brightness catches my attention.
Shading my eyes from the sun,
I look up to see a hummingbird
at the feeder just outside my window.
The rubythroat's sunlit colors bedazzle me!

No matter how many hummingbirds I see,
no matter how many words I write about them,
I never cease to be awestruck
by the iridescence and artistry
of this infinitesimal creature,
this microcosm of wonder,
this jewel of the bird world,
this flying rainbow.

But just as strong is my amazement
that the rubythroat is here at the feeder at all—
for this tiny dynamo of energy
has flown, undaunted,
to the shores of the Gulf,
sped across the waves to the Yucatan—
and back!—on its courageous odyssey.
What mystery! What power!
What infinite glory wrapped in feathers,
radiant color, and motion!

The least I can do is provide a welcoming spot
on the rubythroat's journey back home.

For Further Reading

Ackerman, Diane. "Mute Dancers: How to Watch a Hummingbird."
New York Times Magazine, May 29, 1994.
Adams, George. *Birdscaping Your Garden*. Emmaus, Pa.: Rodale
Press, 1994.
Baker, Robin, ed. *The Mystery of Migration*. New York: Viking Press,
1981.
Bedichek, Roy. *Adventures with a Texas Naturalist*. Austin: University
of Texas Press, 1980.
Bent, Arthur Cleveland. *Life Histories of North American Cuckoos,
Goatsuckers, Hummingbirds, and Their Allies*. U.S. National
Museum Bulletin 176 (1940).
Biel, Timothy Levi. *Zoobooks 2: Hummingbirds*. San Diego, Calif.:
Wildlife Education, 1985.
Dennis, John V. *A Guide to Western Bird Feeding*. Marietta, Ohio:
Bird Watcher's Digest Press, 1991.
Dugdale, Vera. *Album of North American Birds*. Chicago: Rand
McNally & Co., 1967.
Ehrlich, Paul R., David S. Dobkin, and Darryl Wheye. *The Birder's
Handbook: A Field Guide to the Natural History of North American
Birds*. New York: Simon & Schuster, 1988.
Feduccia, Alan. *The Age of Birds*. Cambridge, Mass.: Harvard University
Press, 1980.
Finch, Robert. "The Flower Kissers." *Diversion*, July 1990.
Finlay, J. C., ed. *A Bird-Finding Guide to Canada*. Edmonton:
Hurtig Publishers, 1984.
Forshaw, Joseph, ed. *Encyclopedia of Birds*. New York: Smithmark
Publishers, 1991.
Greenewalt, Crawford H. *Hummingbirds*. Garden City, N.Y.:
American Museum of Natural History, Doubleday & Co., 1960.
———. "Nature's Little Dynamos." In *The Gift of Birds*, ed. H. F.
Robinson. Washington, D.C.: National Wildlife Federation, 1979.
Griffin, Donald R. *Bird Migration*. New York: Dover Publications,
1974.
Gruson, Edward S. *Words for Birds: A Lexicon of North American
Birds with Biographical Notes*. New York: Quadrangle Books, 1972.

[143]

Hainsworth, Reed, and Larry Wolf. "Hovering Hummingbirds."
WildBird 8 (May 1994): 38–41.

Hilton, Bill. "Migration of Ruby-throated Hummingbirds."
WildBird 8 (May 1994): 42–45.

———. *The Piedmont Naturalist.* Vol. 1. York, S.C.: Hilton Pond
Press, 1986.

Holmgren, Virginia C. *The Way of the Hummingbird: In Legend, History
and Today's Gardens.* San Bernardino, Calif.: Capra Press, 1986.

Howell, Steve N. G., and Sophie Webb. *A Guide to the Birds of
Mexico and Northern Central America.* New York: Oxford
University Press, 1995.

Jackson, Greg D. "First Occurrence of Black-chinned Hummingbird
in Alabama." *American Birds* 42 (Winter 1987–1988): 178–179.

Johnsgard, Paul A. *The Hummingbirds of North America.* Washington, D.C.: Smithsonian Institution Press, 1983.

Konrad, Paul. "American Hummingbirds." *Wildbird* 8 (May 1994):
36–37.

Kress, Stephen W. *The Audubon Society Handbook for Birders.* New
York: Charles Scribner's Sons, 1981.

Kress, Stephen W. *The Audubon Society Guide to Attracting Birds.*
New York: Charles Scribner's Sons, 1985.

LaBastille, Anne. "The Rites of Passage." In *The Wonder of Birds.*
Washington, D.C.: National Geographic Society, 1983.

Manry, David E. "Rocky Mountain Triller." *Birder's World* 9 (August
1995): 27–31.

McClung, Robert. "Egrets and the Plume Trade." In *The Gift of
Birds,* ed. H. F. Robinson. Washington, D.C.: National Wildlife
Federation, 1979.

McCracken, Karen Harden. *Connie Hagar: The Life History of a Texas
Birdwatcher.* College Station: Texas A&M University Press, 1986.

McElroy, Thomas P., Jr. *Habitat Guide to Birding.* New York: Alfred
A. Knopf, 1974.

Miller, Richard S. "Why Hummingbirds Hover." *Auk* 102 (October
1985): 722–726.

Newfield, Nancy. "Hummers: Losing Ground." *Bird Watcher's Digest*
13 (July 1991): 62–68.

———. *Louisiana's Hummingbirds.* Baton Rouge: Louisiana Department of Wildlife and Fisheries, Natural Heritage Program, 1993.

Newfield, Nancy, and Barbara Nielsen. *Hummingbird Gardens:
Attracting Nature's Jewels to Your Backyard.* Shelburne, Vt.:
Chapters Publishing, 1996.

Newsom-Brighton, Maryanne. "A Garden Fit for Hummingbirds."
Bird Watcher's Digest 10 (January 1988): 18–25.

Norris, Robert A., Clyde E. Connell, and David W. Johnston.
"Notes on Fall Plumages, Weights, and Fat Condition in the
Ruby-throated Hummingbird." *Wilson Bulletin* 69(2):155–163.

Oberholser, Harry C. *The Bird Life of Texas*. Vol. 1. Austin: University of Texas Press, 1974.

Page, Kack, and Eugene S. Morton. *Lords of the Air*. Washington,
D.C.: Smithsonian Books, 1989.

Pearson, T. Gilbert, ed. *Birds of America*. Garden City, N.Y.: Garden
City Publishing, 1936.

Peterson, Roger Tory, and Edward L. Chalif. *A Field Guide to
Mexican Birds and Adjacent Central America*. Boston:
Houghton Mifflin Co., 1973.

Pettingill, Olin Sewall, Jr. *Ornithology in Laboratory and Field*. 4th
ed. Minneapolis: Burgess Publishing, 1970.

Pollock, Robert. "Summer Hummer." *Birder's World* 5 (October
1991): 30–32.

———. "The Woodland Sweetshop." *Birder's World* 5 (December
1991): 42–43.

Schwetman, Jean. "Nature Notebook: Mantis Can Be Death to Tiny
Birds." *Waco Tribune-Herald*, September 23, 1995.

Shalaway, Scott. "How to Attract Hummingbirds." *WildBird* 8
(May 1994): 46–54.

———. "Understanding Predation and Survival." *WildBird* 9 (July
1995).

Skutch, Alexander F. *The Life of the Hummingbird*. New York:
Crown Publishers, 1973.

———. *Birds Asleep*. Austin: University of Texas Press, 1989.

Snyder, Gordon M. "The Wonders of Bird Navigation." In *The Gift
of Birds,* ed. H. F. Robinson. Washington, D.C.: National
Wildlife Federation, 1979.

Southwick, E. E., and A. K. Southwick. "Energetics of Feeding on
Tree Sap by Ruby-throated Hummingbirds in Michigan."
American Midland Naturalist 104(2):328–334.

Sparling, Dawn. *Hummingbirds Are Fun!* Santa Cruz, Calif.:
Woodsworld, 1973.

Stallcup, Rich. "Cats: A Heavy Toll on Songbirds, a Reversible
Catastrophe." *Observer, Quarterly Journal of the Point Reyes Bird
Observatory*, Spring–Summer 1991.

Stiles, F. Gary, and Alexander F. Skutch. *A Guide to the Birds of Costa Rica*. Ithaca, N.Y.: Comstock Publishing Associates, Cornell University Press, 1989.

Stokes, Donald W., and Lillian Q. Stokes. *A Guide to Bird Behavior*. Vol. 3. Boston: Little, Brown & Co., 1989.

———. *The Hummingbird Book*. Boston: Little, Brown & Co., 1989.

———. "The Beat of a Different Hummer." *Bird Watcher's Digest* 11 (March 1989): 102–108.

———. "Hawks to Hummers." *Bird Watcher's Digest* 12 (September 1989): 108–114.

Swengel, Ann. "How to Find Hummingbirds in the Wild." *Bird Watcher's Digest* 13 (May 1991): 68–75.

Terres, John K. *The Audubon Society Encyclopedia of North American Birds*. New York: Alfred A. Knopf, 1980.

———. *Songbirds in Your Garden*. Chapel Hill, N.C.: Algonquin Books, 1994.

Texas Parks and Wildlife Department. *Nature Tourism in the Lone Star State: Economic Opportunities in Nature*. A report of the State Task Force on Texas Nature Tourism. Austin: Texas Parks and Wildlife Dept., 1995.

Toops, Connie. *Hummingbirds: Jewels in Flight*. Stillwater, Minn.: Voyageur Press, 1992.

Tyrrell, Esther. *Hummingbirds: Their Life and Behavior*. New York: Crown Publishers, 1985.

Tyrrell, Esther, and Robert Tyrrell. "The World's Smallest Bird." *National Geographic* 177 (June 1990): 72–75.

Vosburgh, Pat. "The Fabulous Feather." *Bird Watcher's Digest* 11 (September 1988): 60–64.

Wauer, Roland H. *The Visitor's Guide to the Birds of the Central National Parks: United States and Canada*. Santa Fe, N. Mex.: John Muir Publications, 1994.

Wolf, Larry, and Reed Hainsworth. "Hummingbird Torpor." *WildBird* 9 (May 1995): 44–45.

Womack, Ellie. "Notable Recaptures of Banded Ruby-throated Hummingbirds." *Bulletin of the Oklahoma Ornithological Society*, December 1994: 30–31.

———. "Occurrence of Albinistic Hummingbirds in Oklahoma." *Bulletin of the Oklahoma Ornithological Society* 28 (June 1995): 9–13.